Moving Beyond *Your* Parents' Divorce

Mel Krantzler, Ph.D.
Patricia Biondi Krantzler

Contemporary Books

Chicago   New York   San Francisco   Lisbon   London   Madrid   Mexico City
Milan   New Delhi   San Juan   Seoul   Singapore   Sydney   Toronto

HQ
777
.5
.K7
2003

Library of Congress Cataloging-in-Publication Data

Krantzler, Mel.
    Moving beyond your parents' divorce / Mel Krantzler, Patricia Biondi
Krantzler.
        p.   cm.
    Includes index.
    ISBN 0-07-140248-9 (alk. paper)
    1. Adult children of divorced parents—Psychology.   2. Adult children
of divorced parents—Mental health.   3. Adult children of divorced
parents—Attitudes.   I. Krantzler, Patricia B.   II. Title.

HQ777.5 .K7   2003
306.89—dc21   2002073924

1 2 3 4 5 6 7 8 9 0   AGM/AGM   2 1 0 9 8 7 6 5 4 3

ISBN 0-07-140248-9

McGraw-Hill books are available at special quantity discounts to use as premiums
and sales promotions, or for use in corporate training programs. For more
information, please write to the Director of Special Sales, Professional Publishing,
McGraw-Hill, Two Penn Plaza, New York, NY 10121-2298. Or contact your local
bookstore.

This book is printed on acid-free paper.

To Nora and Julie, Karen and Vickie—the daughters in our lives

Contents

Foreword

Our culture informs us that parents who divorce will inevitably stigmatize their children and they will then have a more difficult time in their long-term emotional and social adjustment. If we believe this myth, we must also support the corollary that children of intact marriages (no matter what the quality of that relationship) will have an easier time in their subsequent emotional and social development, including their own marriages.

In *Moving Beyond Your Parents' Divorce* the Krantzlers successfully challenge this myth by presenting overwhelming evidence that being a child of divorce, in itself, is not the stigmatizing, destructive influence some hold it to be.

The belief that divorce will have a destructive impact on children has gained the status of myth in our society. As such, it is generally unquestioned and is transmitted from one generation to the next. The Krantzlers have been working with divorced and divorcing individuals for three decades. In recent years, they have focused their energies and research on children of divorce. In this book, they argue that the persistent cultural myth about the long-term destructiveness of divorce on children no longer has a basis in fact. They challenge the myth and present a convincing case for us to take a new, benevolent, objective look at children of divorce.

Myth

Myth is a form of social behavior. It does not arise without reason. There is always some basis for the origins of myth, and there is usually some basis for the energy that sustains myth across time.

The myth that children of divorce would incur difficulties as a result of the divorce may have been multidetermined. It may have served as an indirect threat against divorcing. It may have reflected a fear that the tendency to divorce may be transmitted from parent to child. It most probably reflected the obvious fact that children of divorce would lack part of the important parenting that the children of intact unions would receive.

In an era when divorce was the exception, children of divorce stood out in any community. Any difficulty in the development or behavior of a child of divorce could easily be assigned to the fact that this was a child of divorce. Those children of divorce who turned out well could be explained away as the exception that proves the rule.

The myth did not take into account the possibility that some children of divorce could actually do better in their development once free of the stress of a deteriorating and possibly violent marital environment.

The myth may have served to sustain marriages by implying a threat to their offspring if the parents separated or divorced. It may have reflected the vulnerability of married women in the days before community property laws. It may have been a means of enhancing marital stability to conform to religious pronouncements about the nature of marriage and the responsibility of parenting. Divorce was taken as a sign that something was fundamentally wrong with the people involved. Sadly, this negative attitude was carried over to the children of divorce. They were stigmatized. It was widely believed that they could not possibly turn out as well as the children of intact marriages.

De-Mythologizing Children of Divorce

Times have changed. Divorce, once the exception, now impacts almost half of all marriages. Children of divorce, once exceptions in the community, are now common. Family structure has also changed. Single parents and working mothers are now accepted without the stigmatization they would have experienced during the previous century. But what about the children of divorce? Is it still fair to stigmatize them, to have negative expectations for their future development and happiness?

The Krantzlers ask us to dismiss the myth that divorce always has an adverse impact on the emotional and social development of children. They argue their case from their extensive work with families of divorce over the last three decades. They present evidence that some children have developed insights and interpersonal skills simply because of the impact of parental divorce. They suggest that children have an innate resiliency that enables them to not only endure but also actually surmount the challenges presented by parental divorce.

The Krantzlers' case is also strengthened by several factors:

• There is no convincing evidence to support the cultural myth that divorce has a negative impact on the involved children or that children of divorce are not as well-adjusted as children of intact marriages. In fact, for some children the divorce can result in a lessening of stress and a freedom from the discord, tensions, and even violence that predated the actual separation or divorce.

• Children of divorce can become model, happy, productive citizens while children of intact marriages can become outrageous criminals. The successful children of divorce are not simply "the exception that proves the rule" any more than the delinquent children of intact marriages are proof that marriage in itself has a toxic influence on child development.

• Having a divorce in one's background is not the ultimate determining factor in adolescent or adult behavior. This is not meant to minimize the stress of discord and divorce on children. But, as the Krantzlers repeatedly point out, the negative myth about the impact of divorce does not take into account the natural "resiliency" of many children.

During my training in child psychiatry I heard the dictum that, "Children tend to turn out either good or bad to a large extent depending on their parents' fantasies about them." In general, children respond to benevolent expectations just as they are subject to the influence of repeated, hurtful expectations uttered by parents and other significant persons.

We have also been told that no matter how much a child has been abused, they can survive and surmount hardship and stress if, during their formative years, at least one adult proves to be a constant, psychologically nurturing influence for them.

The Influence of Genetics

One of the most interesting developments in recent years has been the relationship of genetic science to behavior. Odd as it may seem, genetics has some relevance to the subject of this book. We know that divorce is generally a stressful event or series of events in a family. We also know from the extensive work of the Krantzlers that divorce does not produce consistently adverse effects on all persons involved, including children.

What other factors must be taken into account in determining the development and later behavior of children of divorce? We cannot exclude the possibility that genetic factors play a role in the development of children, whether or not they are exposed to the stress of divorce. In fact, genetic factors may play a role in what is referred to in this book as "resiliency."

Are some children more "resilient" than others? To be more specific, are some children more likely to surmount adverse circumstances than others, to remain apparently unaffected by adversity while others are less able to surmount adverse circumstances? A thirty-year, longitudinal study of 442 white, male New Zealanders, starting from the time of birth, was reported in August 2002 by Caspi and colleagues in the journal *Science*. These authors offer strong evidence for a genetic determinant of behavior, at least in white males who had been neglected and abused during childhood.

The study provides evidence for why some children are resilient while others are adversely impacted by neglect and abuse as evident in their subsequent behavior. The determining factor is a gene located on the X (male) chromosome that produces an enzyme, monoamine oxidase-A (MAOA). The enzyme MAOA degrades naturally occurring neurotransmitters like serotonin and dopamine. There are two varieties of the gene on the X chromosome: one that results in high levels of MAOA and the other in low amounts. Earlier studies in mice showed low MAOA to be linked to aggressive behavior, as did one study in human subjects. In the journal *Nature* in 2002, Gross and his research team demonstrated the action of the serotonin receptor, 1-A, in the development of anxiety-like behavior in the adult. Other studies, including Belzung's, printed in *Behavioral Pharmacology* in 2001, demonstrate the relationship between genetics and the pharmacological effects of anxiolytics.

Fifty-five subjects in the study had low levels of MAOA. This group with low MAOA was twice as likely as their high-level MAOA to have engaged in persistent fighting, bullying, theft, cruelty, and vandalism during adolescence. The low MAOA group was also more likely to have been convicted of a crime than their high level MAOA counterparts who had also been abused or neglected. Low MAOA in the absence of abuse does not in itself increase the risk of later delinquency or criminal behavior. Thus, there is no "genetic determinism" that can be traced to levels of MAOA. The predisposition to later disturbed behavior is multidetermined. As contributing author Terrie Moffit, from Kings's College London, England, states, "Genes can moderate children's sensitivity to environmental insults."

Another researcher from King's College, Ian Craig, said "Maltreatment seems to cause lasting changes in brain chemistry. He also suggests that genetic variation in levels of MAOA "may partly explain why not all victims of maltreatment grow up to victimize others; some genotypes (those that lead to high levels of MAOA) may promote resistance to trauma."

In a recent 2002 review in *New England Journal of Medicine* of the long-term effects of early genetic influences on behavior, Dr. Freedman stated that the research presently does not answer the question of whether the effect of an experience on the mouse or genetically controlled development determines its adult behavior. He further states, "A full answer might reveal interesting interactions, such as a possible interaction between adverse experience and genetically determined biologic mechanisms that alters neuronal development. Indeed, the introduction of genetic techniques into behavioral science makes research into such questions more feasible than it has previously been."

The "Snickett" Factor

A series of books for children written by Lemony Snickett bears the title, "A Series of Unfortunate Events." The first volume is titled, *The Bad Beginning*. The books in this series mock the familiar fairy tale ending, "and they all lived happily ever after." Volume one warns the juvenile reader that there is no happy ending, no happy beginning and "very few happy things in the middle." On page eight the children are told "Your parents . . . have perished in a terrible fire." The strange humor in these books, if it is anything, is testimony to the resiliency of children. They somehow survive a series of misadventures to face an uncertain future in which they are obviously vulnerable. The unanticipated popularity of the Lemony Snickett books, published by Harper-Collins, is paralleled in a popular comedy movie, *The Royal Tenenbaums*, that focuses on the folly of adults and the vulnerability of children. Loss and death are common themes in the Snickett books and in the Tenenbaum movie. Adults are portrayed as inconstant and unreliable, children as vulnerable, resourceful, and resilient. The perverse content of the books and the movie are in contrast to the benevolent outcome of children's books that follow the customary fairy-tale theme in which the protagonist somehow surmounts tragedy and all ends well. Snickett themes, in their harsh portrayal of a child's world, take us back to fairy tales of the nineteenth century when death was a common theme and the obvious intent of the story was to leave the young reader with a moralizing message intended to channel future behavior. The Snickett books and the Tenenbaum movie reflect a sea change in their portrayal of the ability of children to survive and surmount a succession of tragedies. They are not stigmatized as the children of divorce are. Instead, they are seen as responsible realists who work to improve their situation no matter what happens to the significant adults in their lives.

Lessons from Hospice

One of the major factors motivating me to develop a hospice program during the early 1970s was my observation of the impact of the death of a parent on children I was treating in my practice (child psychiatry). The death of a parent or sibling resulted in a wide spectrum of behavioral changes in children depending on their age, their basic psychological health, and a host of other factors. Over the past thirty years I have come to know hundreds of families because of my work with a member of the family who was dying. In many instances I visited the homes over a period of months and came to know the children quite well. In fact, I still hear from some of them decades after the death of a parent.

My observations regarding the long-range impact of death on the development of children parallels the observations of the Krantzlers on the development of children of divorce. In brief, the short-term impact may be quite stressful, but the long-term impact is not necessarily bleak. I subscribe to the dictum of Erik Erikson, who wrote in 1974's *Childhood and Society* that, "grief, successfully handled, can serve as the focus for new social and psychological growth."

What do we mean by the term, "successfully handled"? Most importantly, there is no magic. The resolution of grief takes time.

There is a lot of information to process, a lot of uncertainty to resolve, and a great deal of rearrangement of one's life. In the long term there will be a new awareness of relationships, an awareness of one's finity, a realignment of objectives, and an eventual reassessment of priorities. This takes time and is more likely to occur after the environment begins to stabilize.

Children tend to model their behavior on that of significant adults. I recall the clearest example of how this works. About twenty years ago a young father died in his home. We knew the family from numerous earlier visits. The father died during the night when the three small children were sleeping in their beds. We suggested to the mother that the children have an opportunity to see their father and to say their "goodbyes" before the body was removed to the funeral home. We carried the two youngest children to see their father. The oldest, a son, walked. The children stood at the bedside to see and say "goodbye" to their father. After some very moving words and some tears the son looked up at his mother and asked, "Are you all right, Mom?" When she replied that she was "all right," the son responded, "Then I am all right, too."

For children to even begin to make a successful adjustment to a major family disruption like death or divorce, they need to know several things. They may not always ask clear questions as the young boy did in the case cited above.

In the first place, children need to know that they will be cared for, no matter what. They need to know that they did not cause the problem. They need to know that the same problem will not necessarily occur to them when they reach the same age as the person who died or who left because of divorce. They need someone they can confide in, someone who can answer their questions, someone who will be a consistent and steady presence in their lives.

Moving Beyond Your Parents' Divorce offers no Pollyanna advice. It does not minimize the distress divorce brings to all concerned. But instead of accepting the outdated myth that divorce always stigmatizes children, it offers evidence that the distress of divorce can serve as a stimulus for the new social and psychological growth that we have observed in children who have had to deal with the untimely death of a parent. The myth about children of divorce needs to be put behind us. In its place, the Krantzlers offer the message that children have an innate resilience that will enable them to transcend not only divorce of their parents, but most stressful situations that come their way.

—WILLIAM M. LAMERS JR., M.D.

Acknowledgments

Without the total willingness of the men and women in our adult children of divorce groups to honestly share their experiences with the readers of this book, it would not have been possible to be written. Their wish to help other adult children of divorce has been their motivating factor. Our gratitude to them is more than words alone can fully express.

We also wish to thank our editor, Judith McCarthy, for her insightful editorial suggestions that have creatively enhanced the contents of this book.

Our agent, Richard Curtis, enthusiastically supported our writing endeavors. His belief in the value of our work was a major spur to its completion. Our thanks for his reinforcement.

Introduction

Self-Empowerment for Adult Children of Divorce

This book is an unqualified, nonapologetic defense of adult children of divorce. It is the first of its kind, because other books on this subject have been patronizing or negatively judgmental, or they proclaim that one never really heals from the "disaster" of their parents' divorce during his or her entire lifetime.

Our book is not only a defense of adult children of divorce and younger children living in divorce households, but it is also designed to help anyone who struggles with feelings of ambivalence about his or her legacy of being a product of divorced parents. We also want to reassure parents anticipating or experiencing divorce that they needn't feel that they are victimizing their children by taking such action. There is a road ahead in your life to prevent permanent harm to your children, and we will chart that road with prescriptive advice in this book.

The media continue to proliferate an enormous amount of misleading information and negative value judgments. Because of this, people feel guilty about being children of divorce, and their parents believe that their divorce will inevitably make second-class citizens out of their children. To list all of the media hype and pundits who continue to reiterate with the authority of ignorance (well-intentioned or otherwise) that divorce inevitably damages children for life would take up all of the pages of this book. When has it been stated on any major television show ("The

Oprah Show," "Good Morning America," or "Today") or reported in any weekly magazine (*Time* or *Newsweek*) that divorce is anything other than a major tragedy for children, and that children of divorce, as well as their parents, can respond creatively and prevent such a tragedy from happening? The questions answer themselves.

Our book affirms that the effect of divorce can be no more traumatic than any other serious event in a child's experience—be it severe illness, physical injury, or disability or religious or social discrimination, which can occur in so-called "intact" families as well as in divorced households. In fact, the resilience and competency of children of divorce often exceed the achievements of children from many "intact" households that may be dysfunctional in the extreme. This conclusion is based on the experiences of thousands of divorced parents and their children (children of all ages from preadolescents to adults in their fifties) who we have counseled during the past three decades, and these experiences will be shared with you in this book.

We are both psychological counselors who have established children of divorce research groups over the past three decades at our Creative Divorce, Love & Marriage Counseling Center located in San Rafael, California. When we wrote *Creative Divorce* more than two decades ago, divorce was still considered a sign of personal failure, and the concept of divorce as a "creative" experience was considered a weird aberration. It is encouraging to note that this is no longer the case. *Creative Divorce* ran against the conventional wisdom of its time that said divorce was a sin and an inevitable disaster. But divorced people then were hungry for realistic hope to counter this dark view of divorce. *Creative Divorce* provided that hope and became the only book at that time to respond to that need. (It has sold more than three million copies and has been published in a number of different languages.)

Indeed, millions of men and women are now trying to make their divorce a creative experience, which means learning from their past mistakes rather than repeating them. However, very little progress has been made in the arena of adult children of divorce. They remain demeaned as a stereotyped group, and little attention has been paid in the media to the positive benefits they can derive by prevailing over their parents' divorce, even when such a divorce is dysfunctional.

Our book is more than the product of our extensive research: it is also a personal labor of love. Both of us have counseled people of all ages in all types of relationships, and because we ourselves were divorced (Mel included his own divorce experience in *Creative Divorce* and his remarriage to Pat in *Learning to Love Again*), and because we each had two daughters in their early teens from our first marriages when we remarried, we have had a special interest in this subject. It was the motivating force for creating our ongoing adult children of divorce groups. Our children—all adult children of divorce—are married now and have children of their own. They lead normal, productive lives, and so do their children. Our research, as well as our personal experience, reveals that this development is more the rule rather than the exception. A wealth of evidence arises from our ongoing adult children of divorce groups, which we will share with you in subsequent chapters. The men and women in our groups range in age from twenty-one to fifty-eight and are multicultural. The groups also include bisexual and homosexual men and women who grew up in divorced households. They too have created healthy and constructive adult lives for themselves and are proud of their achievements.

Before we discuss the achievements of adult children of divorce (ACDs), we believe it is of primary importance to destroy the destructive myths about them that still pervade in our society and create unnecessary roadblocks that could inhibit efforts to achieve their maximum potential. Our book is designed to help you identify those roadblocks and to indicate the ways in which they can be overcome. The men and women that we describe in this book have triumphed over their own adversities as ACDs, and they are typical people with typical problems that arose from their own parents' divorce. You may see yourself in some of them.

Many real issues in our society—that have no connection with divorce—can and do destroy peoples' lives, such as the fact that *44 percent of all Americans today have no health insurance.* The sound of silence emerges from the media about how in 1992, 38 percent of Americans were without health insurance, while 16 percent more Americans were added to those in the next decade. The test of our nation's prosperity and wellness should be how our society takes care of all of its children. Attention needs to be paid to the excessive harm caused to children—and their parents—by conditions other than divorce. As Jack Levine, National Association of Child Advocates board member, in a CNN interview on December 5, 1999, stated: "We know that our children are suffering from great damage as a result of their parents, frankly, not being able to make ends meet in many, many cases. A nation that has one-fifth of its children—one in five—without the means to make ends meet and access to health care is not only an economic problem, but we think it's a national shame."

Now that 78 million baby boomers have become or are approaching fifty, they are beginning to experience the personal fears and insecurities of becoming "old," something they had always believed happened to "others," not themselves. The future for them and their children—whether they are married or divorced—is fraught with insecurity. For the millions without health insurance and without job security, they indeed have reason to worry about who will need them or feed them. Their own aged parents are already a matter of serious concern, because the fastest growing segment of our population is the eighty-five-plus generation. They need adequate care, yet decent nursing care costs $40,000 a year for starters. Now, seven million seniors depend on twenty-four-hour, bedside-assistance caregivers in the nursing home industry. *By the year 2020, fourteen million will need such care.* The care they now receive is a national scandal. They receive, for the most part, assistance from overworked and underpaid caregivers who earn starting pay of $7.00 an hour on the average. And workers with thirty years service are likely to receive no more than $10.20 an hour!

It is in this social and economic context that the demeaning and the disparagement of ACDs occur. Why else would the falsehoods about this major segment of our population continue to be repeated from the middle of the twentieth century until today? It is a very potent smokescreen, because it blames the victim rather than the victimizer for all of the problems the millions of men and women who grew up in divorced households are facing today. When ACDs are told that they are "damaged" and that only they themselves and their parents are responsible for the problems they face, it's easy to distract the public from attending to and solving such problems as the lack of decent jobs at decent pay, poor or nonexistent day-care centers, inadequate or nonexistent health care, which are just a few of the problems the majority of our population—not only ACDs—have to contend with.

The objective of our book is to empower children of divorce—adult and otherwise—and to reinforce their self-esteem so they can make positive things happen in their lives. The groundwork for children of divorce becoming successful adults resides in the way their parents handle their divorce. When parents view their divorce as an opportunity for personal growth—rather than as a disaster in which they see themselves as victims or as vengeful attackers of their former "wicked" marriage partner—they become positive role models for their children. They demonstrate to their children that the adversities of divorce are challenges in life that can be overcome, rather than as events that will destroy any possibility of future happiness. We have called this approach to divorce *creative divorce* and identified the components of such a divorce in two books, *Creative Divorce* and *The New Creative Divorce*.

This new book can be considered a sequel to those two books. It focuses on the quality of life children of divorce achieve, rather than on their parents' lives, which our previous books did. However, our basic findings about how divorced couples can practice a creative divorce are included in this book, because the legacy of how effectively children of divorce can cope with the problems arising from *their* upbringing will be determined to a great extent by how their parents handled the divorce. A creative divorce will nourish the ability of children of divorce to become high achievers, while a bitter, vengeful divorce can inhibit their potential for a successful life. However, because children in general possess enormous resilience, we also present many examples of children of divorce triumphing over the vengeful, bitter divorces many couples still exhibit.

We invite you as a reader concerned about these issues to view our findings, our guidelines, and our prescriptive advice as attempts on our part to provide the information that can help you enhance the quality of your own life. The successful lives of the many adult children of divorce that we have detailed here are role models of accomplishments by men and women who are typical, rather than exceptional, people. Our book is an action-oriented book, designed to empower readers to take personal responsibility to make positive things happen in the arena of their divorce experiences. It is also a how-to-see-it book, inviting readers to take a new, more realistic, hopeful view of children of divorce. Because more than one million children each year live in newly divorced households, we believe nothing can be more helpful and enriching to those parents and their children than to incorporate realistic, practical hope in their lives to counteract the conventional wisdom that was telling them their future would consist only of despair and failure.

An old Chinese proverb states, "It is better to light a single candle than to curse the darkness a thousand times."

This book is our effort to light that candle.

1

The Stereotype of Adult Children of Divorce
The Myth and the Reality

They were two teenage boys, ages seventeen and eighteen, who grew up in a prosperous small city. Each lived in a very nice home, went to an affluent high school, and had upright, law-abiding parents. The two boys never experienced any economic deprivation; they had all the toys and trinkets and cars they desired. Their parents were "nice people" who never abused them and had status in their community: one father was retired from the Air Force; the other was a former geophysicist who ran a mortgage company and whose wife was an administrator in a small college.

The two boys lived in stable households; their parents were in long-term marriages in which neighbors never heard any complaints about their behavior. The consensus was that they were "good people."

In another scenario, there was a boy who was an only child who never met his father. His mother suffered from schizophrenia and was put into a psychiatric hospital when the boy was six years old. The boy was placed in a Catholic orphanage, where he stayed for four years and after that, for the most part, had to fend for himself.

If we used conventional wisdom to predict the outcome of these children once they reached adulthood, the prognostication would be obvious: the two children growing up in a prosperous environment would become two praiseworthy members of whatever community they would live in.

On the other hand, the boy who was tossed through his childhood like a leaf in a storm would be considered a permanent loser, lucky to be alive when he turned old enough to vote, but more likely he would be dead or in jail by that time.

The prediction would be right about a death before adulthood. But it would be totally wrong about who would be dead. Rather than one person dying at no later than age eighteen, there were two—and they were the two boys who grew up in the environment of affluence and intact marriages that we noted above.

They were eighteen-year-old Eric Harris and seventeen-year-old Dylan Klebold, the two students who arrived at Columbine High School in Littleton, Colorado, at lunchtime on April 20, 1999, with guns in hand. They killed twelve of their fellow students and one teacher and wounded twenty-three other students. They then turned the guns on themselves and committed suicide. It subsequently turned out they had stored enough explosives to blow up the high school.

But the poverty-stricken child living in an economically deprived area of New York City grew up to become one of our country's most famous novelists. He is Robert Stone, author of *Damascus Gate*, *Children of Light*, and *Dog Soldiers* among other noted books. He has said that it was "curious luck" to have been raised by his schizophrenic mother. "It gave me tremendous advantage in understanding the relationship of language to reality. I had to sort out causality for myself."

In other words, in these scenarios, the "lucky" person is the person with the disadvantaged background; the unlucky losers were the two adolescents who grew up with the kind of advantages people brag about. Robert Stone had used his background of adversity as a training ground for becoming a very important writer. On the other hand, Eric Harris and Dylan Klebold created a hell on earth for themselves that resulted in murder and suicide.

Of course, we are not generalizing, saying that all "single parent" families are wonderful and that all nondivorced parents in long-term marriages nurture their children into monsterhood. Nor are we saying that growing up deprived economically and socially in unsafe neighborhoods is a gift a person should be grateful to receive. Far from it. Our point in contrasting the two ways of life is to demonstrate the absurdity of generalizing about *all* married households or *all* divorced households from selected examples. Just as marriages comes in all shapes and sizes—good, bad, indifferent, or horrible—divorces also comes in all shapes and sizes ranging from negative to positive.

Yet the old twentieth-century stereotypes continue to persist into this new millennium. We constantly hear messages that marriage is "always good" and divorce "always bad" when it comes to nurturing children. That imprinting on the general public's mind leads to the subsequent conclusion that children will grow up to be wholesome adults if they had parents who never divorced, while children of divorce will develop into defective grownups. Of course, exceptions to these absurd stereotypes appear in the media, but they are few and far between. And incidents like the Columbine High School tragedy are reported always as "exceptions" to the general rule and consequently to be discounted as undermining these stereotypes.

However, more than enough scientific and anecdotal information is available—through a modest amount of research on the Internet and in libraries—to demonstrate the falsity of these stereotypes. There are no such things as *a* divorce or *a* child of divorce. Instead, there are many variations of divorce and the consequences of those variations, as well as many different types of children of divorce that arise. How parents and children deal with their divorce experiences—positively or negatively—will be shaped to a considerable extent by the kind of divorce that they must cope with. We will share with you the major divorce variations in the next few pages.

In our Creative Divorce, Love & Marriage Counseling Center, we have counseled thousands of couples who seek our advice about separating. We have yet to find two couples whose divorces are identical. In other words, there are *divorces*, not *divorce*.

Each couple comes to us with his and her unique form of pain and fantasies about what might happen after the one household they share will become two separate places possibly in two different communities. We could list hundreds of different types of divorces, but that would cause this book to be as long as *War and Peace*. We will list, instead, the divorce variations that are most typical. But even in these typical kinds of formations, each couple acts out the consequences of spousal separation in a way unique to that couple.

Contrary to popular belief, divorce does not begin when an attorney is sought out. It may even begin in one's feelings that first week of a marriage that lasts ten or twenty years. It is also a divorce when a person is alienated in his or her feelings and no longer considers the partner to be the number-one person in his or her life (e.g., the person one loves the most, trusts the most, and who is one's very best friend who can always be counted on to be concerned about a wife's or husband's personal welfare). The legal piece of paper says it is a marriage, but it is a divorce without labeling it as such. Here are some of the major divorce variations we have witnessed in our counseling practice.

The After-the-Wedding-Ceremony Divorce

This is the discovery that each of you made a terrible mistake. Temperamentally, you are grossly mismatched, the sex is disappointing, and value differences are fundamental. Ashamed to acknowledge the "mistake," a couple may live together for many years before seeking out an attorney.

The Alienation Divorce

Apathy and boredom are the opposites of love. When a person simply doesn't give a damn about his or her spouse and neither wishes to engage in sex or even take a night out together, staying together becomes a choice between a greater inconvenience (fear of a loss of income through a legal divorce, loss of the creature comforts of home life) and the lesser inconvenience of living in boredom. Eventually the boredom becomes intolerable—but that might occur half a dozen years or longer after the marriage license was signed.

The "I Am King (or Queen) of the Castle" Divorce

Many couples are trapped in a dictatorship, held captive in the belief by either the husband or wife that he or she who earns the most money is entitled to make all the major family decisions unilaterally. Either implied or spoken, that spouse will demand to make the decisions on how to parent, how to budget, when to buy a house or car, and what kinds of furniture to buy. The marriage snaps into court when the powerless partner can no longer stand the pressure of this loveless relationship.

The Power-Struggle Divorce

From the start of living together, each spouse is locked into an "I'd rather be right than be happy" frame of mind. Both are unbudgeable. Each believes he or she is right and the spouse is wrong on any bone of contention. It can be as minor as "You deliberately leave the toilet seat up when I need it to be down." There is no room for error: each believes he or she is a saint, and his or her partner is invariably the sinner. With no room for compassion, compromise, or forgiveness, who can call this a marriage? It is simply a legal divorce waiting to happen.

The Injustice-Collecting Divorce

In this marriage that becomes a divorce, a volcano-size amount of internalized unspoken resentment and anger against one's partner for the alleged harm he or she has inflicted, is stored for years until it erupts in a divorce attorney's office. (We have heard, once the decision to legally divorce happened, a spouse bitterly accused his wife of deliberately making him thick pancakes for the past fifteen years when she knew he liked them thin. She replied, "This is the first time you told me that! I'm not a mind reader. I would have made you thin pancakes, it was no big deal. But that's what you were like, always silent, always sulking!")

The Family-Triangle Divorce

This is when one partner can't sever the close, child-based union to the parents after the marriage. It's more often, but not always, the wife. So, instead of being married to her husband, she remains "married" to her family. It's her mother or father that she turns to for advice, rather than her husband. When her parents insist she and her husband visit every week for a Sunday dinner, her husband cannot change her mind that they should nurture their own relationship at least occasionally, because Sunday is their only free day together. If her child-based sense of family obligation is never superceded by an adult relationship in which she sets limits to her parents' demands on her marital life, her marriage, in the emotional sense, will never be consummated with her husband. Instead, he most likely will consummate a legal divorce.

The Sexual-Betrayal Divorce

People marry because they want someone to be the number-one person in their lives—a person whom they will love the most, who will be their very best friend, and whom they can trust the most. Nothing can erode that love and friendship and can destroy that trust more than becoming involved in extramarital affairs. Once that trust is broken and suspicion takes its place, the marriage will be very difficult to maintain. Even if a couple does not legally divorce when an affair is discovered, the cloud of mistrust persists, and the damaged marriage becomes the equivalent of a permanent separation with two people becoming lonelier than one while living in the same house.

The Bisexual Divorce

It is not as exceptional as it once was thought to be that a couple will get married, have children, and then later in the marriage (frequently in one's middle thirties or early forties) realize that he or she might feel a greater attraction or love for someone of the same sex. Bisexuality is an acknowledged sexual fact, not a disease. It can and usually does shatter a marriage relationship. A husband or wife can be struggling with his or her bisexual feelings for many years before an actual legal break takes place. During that time, the marriage itself can become a place of mixed signals, ambiguous feelings, and ambivalent actions in which neither spouse feels loved or wanted. The legal divorce becomes the piece of paper that reaffirms what has occurred over many years.

The "My Career Comes First" Divorce

In our society, two-career marriages have become the norm, rather than the exception. While this brings in income to obtain the necessities of life, it can and does create new problems and tensions in a marriage. There is a tendency to become so obsessed with one's personal status and career advancement possibilities, that all other aspects of family life become neglected. And if a career move requires the family to be uprooted to another city or state, as demanded by a spouse, his or her partner might furiously object. And should the move take place in spite of the objection, a sea of resentment can be created that will eventually drown the marriage. "You're married to your job, not me!" is a common complaint we hear from our clients.

The "My Future Is My Past" Divorce

Our society brainwashes us to believe you are a personal failure if you are not a millionaire by the time you are thirty or forty.

This nonsense is internalized by all too many married men and women, who become depressed and view themselves as personal failures when they reach forty or fifty, because they are neither wealthy nor young anymore. Believing they are trapped in a nowhere life, they isolate themselves from their spouses and their children. They live in the same house with them, but they are really living with regret and self-pity. They may never get a legal divorce, but their spouses and children feel they are living in a divorce rather than a fulfilling marriage.

The Drug-Addiction Divorce

This is the marriage in which the turn-on comes from drug addiction rather than from a spouse. The greatest drug addiction in our society is alcohol, yet we continually talk about it as if it were separate from drugs like heroin, cocaine, crack, LSD, or ecstasy. In fact, alcohol is the most lethal of all these "recreational" drugs. There are twenty million problem drinkers in our country (in contrast to a small fraction of that number for all other recreational drugs combined). Alcohol destroys marriages, because it becomes the third party in the relationship; the spouse's true love is a bottle of liquor rather than a family. As long as the spouse continues to drench him- or herself in alcohol, it is the marriage that drowns: the divorce has already occurred.

The "I Never Wanted Children" Divorce

When one spouse wants to have children and the other spouse doesn't but agrees anyway to have peace in the family, the stage is set for disaster. If the spouse who never wanted children doesn't mellow out and change that attitude after the children are born, the children will feel like they are living in a one-parent household and will develop low self-esteem. The children will feel unloved and therefore unlovable. The couple will live on a collision course masquerading as a marriage, with each resenting the other, because each of them continues to have different feelings about their children.

The "My Hobby Is My Spouse" Divorce

When there is a failure to resolve crucial issues in a marriage, one frequent alternative is to love the hobby of your choice instead of the person you married. It could also be a self-isolation passion for browsing the Web, classic cars, TV, sports, gambling, pornographic books, or working on carpentry projects. The list is endless, only limited by the imagination of the person who uses noninvolvement in family life as an escape hatch from building up a constructive relationship with one's spouse and children. This preference for things in place of people creates a family relationship in which living together is really living apart from each other.

The "Sex Is Everything" Divorce

When a spouse believes love means daily intercourse, and every other aspect of the marriage is of secondary importance, resentments accumulate like grains of sand that can become a mountain the longer one persists in this fantasy. For fantasy it is, the product of overdosing on media images of what love is supposed to be about. The "sex is everything" attitude inevitably leads to the highway of the "marriage is nothing." Your partner will resent your sexual timetable demands if he or she has a different desire or nondesire for sex at the time you require it. Should you feel that such rejection is a sign that love has disappeared from your relationships, the stage is set for a journey from "sex is everything" to the "marriage is nothing."

These are just a few of the very many examples we have observed in our three decades of counseling practice of marriages that are really divorces-in-progress. They are, alas, too typical and occur when couples fail to divorce themselves from their unskillful behaviors that perpetuate their alienation from each other.

Positive Approaches to Divorce

However, there are encouraging signs that more and more couples who divorce are seeking out good divorce counselors because they love their children, even if they no longer love each other. They wish to be advised as to how to act in the best interests of their children now that two households are taking the place of one. We have detailed how they learn to act skillfully in the best interests of their children (and also in their own best interests) in our previous books, *Creative Divorce*, *Learning to Love Again*, *The New Creative Divorce*, and *Divorcing*.

These are the parents who learn to set aside their alienation from each other to recognize that their children love *both* mother and father, even though they themselves now may dislike each other. Because that is the case, both the ex-husband and ex-wife will then set aside their anger, resentment, hostility, bitterness, and/or hatred of each other (which usually escalates in the early stages of their breakup) when it comes to dealing constructively with the children. The parents may continue to feel permanently alienated from each other (that's why they divorced) but still love their children and have their best interests at heart.

Such parents tell their children that only parents get divorced, but children will be loved forever and can never be divorced. This is true even when parents remarry—ongoing cooperation between divorced parents will continue in their children's best interests. For this kind of nurturing of their children to occur, flexible, agreed-upon visitation rights; adequate child-support payments; and educational support through college are essential. The children should never become weapons that one parent uses to hurt his or her ex-spouse, such as denying visitation rights when a parent is scheduled to pick up the children or telling a child to spy on one's ex to find out who he or she is now dating.

The parents we counsel who cooperate with each other learn never to bad-mouth one's ex-spouse to one's child (e.g., "You see, your father was late in his child support payment, he's so rotten!" or "Your mother is a no-good slut."). Such bad-mouthing undermines a child's self-image. After all, the child was created by *both* parents. So the child becomes fearful, thinking, "If my mom thinks my dad is rotten, then half of me also must be rotten, because I'm 50 percent created by my dad." The same eroding of the child's self-image takes place should the father disparage the mother in the child's presence.

Couples who divorce and learn to operate in their children's best interests can become successful parents. Despite losing their marriage, they can win the lifetime love and respect of their children. This is something that may never have been possible when they were living together.

However, the divorced couples who do not attempt to learn from their past negative ways of relating are condemned to repeat the past rather than transcend it. In all of the divorces that really masqueraded as marriages that we listed, their actual legal divorce simply became a continuation of their marriage if they did not revise their outlook on life. In their legal divorce, they escalated their alienation from each other by allowing their desire for vengeance to overwhelm them. The desire to pay back, to get even, to hurt, or to harm or kill one's ex-spouse can become obsessive. A random check of your local newspaper reveals, year after year, reports of an enraged ex-spouse murdering his or her former partner, creating endless lawsuits that only benefit the lawyers in the case, setting an ex-spouse's house on fire, or slashing the tires of a car. These are hardly the kind of role models for their children to emulate. It is a tribute to the abilities of most ACDs that they have prevailed over such sordid behavior rather than live in misery. We will be presenting many real life stories to this effect in subsequent chapters.

Avoiding Vengefulness

In our research with ACDs, we asked them what disturbed them the most about their parents' actions after the divorce. The consensus was that the ongoing desire for vengeance—to make one's ex-spouse "pay" for all of the alleged harm that he or she inflicted—was the most disturbing quality that they had hoped and prayed their parents would eliminate from their lives. The sentence that sums up these ACDs' attitude was, "I wish they could have been nicer to each other rather than so vengeful."

We can recall what attorney Melvin Belli—a dear departed friend of ours who had been divorced four times—told us about how vengeance damaged his relationships with his children and himself. We give his story to each of our clients who are divorcing as an educational tool.

If I had it to do over again, here is how I would handle my divorces. I would not voice my bitterness, anger, and feelings of rejection to the world. I remember how clever I thought I was when I made smart-aleck, sarcastic cracks to the press about my soon-to-be ex-wife. And I thought I was being clever when I paid $3,500 to my ex-wife's attorney by sending him the money in two sacks of small change. It made me feel self-righteous at the time but left a legacy of bitterness and hostility that enveloped me and my ex-wife like a black cloud for years long after the divorce. In fact, I haven't seen or heard from my first wife to this day and am not proud of that situation.

I would be kinder. Being kind, not vengeful or permanently bitter, toward your ex-spouse will enable you to feel better about yourself and to lead to a happier life as a single person, rather than with a permanent scowl and a grudge against the world.

As a general principle, the way you act toward your ex-spouse will determine whether or not you will be scarred with hate and vengefulness or feel renewed as a better person, and this is something you should be seriously concerned about. Today, I would be more attentive to how divorce would affect my children and try to minimize the pain, anxiety, confusion, uncertainty, and estrangement. Every missile you hurl has a homing device, and it will hurt not only you but your children. The mutual bitterness between my first wife and me resulted in the very thing I feared the most—my loss of a father connection with my first four children for many years, although my relationship is good with them now. But how much needless pain I endured by allowing my bitter feelings about the divorce to keep me from being more attentive to my children in those early years of their lives. And how much I alienated my children. I did not make that mistake with my child Caesar. I let go of vengeance, my ex and I agreed about fair visitation rights, and I made a point of being alert to Caesar's needs when he was a child. The result has been a happy relationship with my son, although I must admit I'm a somewhat indulgent parent. (And, he's a very independent person and a lawyer now!)

Out of my own experience, I advise my clients (no matter how much the parents may dislike each other at the time they are divorcing) to cool their anger toward each other when they are with their children and to say to them, "Daddy and Mommy love both of you. You're our children forever, so if we do get a divorce it only means that Daddy won't be living here but somewhere nearby and will see you regularly, will go to school with you, will take you to church, will read with you, and you will go over to his new home and enjoy the time spent with him."

Don't ever vilify or criticize your spouse in front of the children. Though they may seem to side with you, they will be so bewildered and traumatized that they won't know what to do or where to go. They will resent someone talking negatively about their father or their mother. Tell them what to say at school, to their teachers, to their ministers, and to others.

If I had it to do over again, I would lead a more balanced family life that might prevent a divorce. I think that in all my four divorces, the prime factor was not enough time at home and too much time at the office. I love my work, and because

I was so intensely involved in it, I failed to see the problems that were developing at home, so I never dealt with them. Well, those problems don't go away just because you don't attend to them; instead, they continue to accumulate until they are insurmountable.

I hope you will first remember me as a person who has experienced many a dark night of the soul, as you may now be doing. But also remember me as a person who knows that you can, with proper guidance, turn that dark night into a sunny morning.

Each Adult Child of Divorce Is Unique

Just as there is no such thing as one of a kind "divorce," as we have demonstrated in this chapter, there is no such thing as one of a kind adult child of divorce. Instead, there are individual divorces and individual children who grew up to be ACDs.

In the same sense, there is no such thing as "marriage," but there are individual marriages. Each relationship needs to be understood and evaluated on its own merit. Otherwise, we will create generalizations that will lead us to false conclusions. For example, to say all marriages are "good" ignores the millions that are poor to miserable. To say all divorces are "bad" is to ignore the positive achievements of the many who divorce because of drug addiction or physical or emotional abuse by a spouse who would destroy their lives if they continued to stay together. And to say that all ACDs were "losers" in love and in the world of work is to overlook the millions who are prevailers, who succeed in love and in a career, as we will detail in subsequent chapters.

The most unjust, false attack directed against all adult children of divorce is the allegation that divorce harms children for life, and that a child of any age is doomed to pay for his or her parents' "sins of divorce" for the rest of his or her life. Divorce is conceived of as a hot branding iron that once imprinted on a child leaves a horrible scar for life. This type of attack leaves no room for variations. It implies or states openly that all divorces do this to all children. For at least three decades, highly unquestionable "scientific" data by alleged "authorities" have been used to "prove" this alleged fact. We had hoped this nonsense would be laid to rest along with the twentieth century. But that isn't the case. An article appeared in the conservative magazine *The National Review* titled "Deadly Divorce." It's subtitle reads: "Divorce can be hazardous to your health—and the health of those around you." It is not written by a specialist in interpersonal relationships but by "a professor of politics at Princeton." It did not appear thirty years ago. It was published April 7, 1997. Shining in all its scarlet-letter glory was the generalized word "divorce." The article doesn't say it is referring to "some" divorces (which would be true) but all divorces (which is false). The best short statement on this subject we have seen was a comment in the *New York Times* letter department, published on December 31, 1995, which observed:

"Blaming children's problems on a megalith called 'Divorce' is a bit like stating that cancer is caused by chemotherapy. Neither divorce nor chemotherapy is a step people hope to have to take in their lives, but each may be the healthiest option in a given situation."

It was written by George Dornfeld, president, Family and Divorce Mediation Council of Greater New York—a person who has hands-on experience with the widest variety of divorcing families, rather than someone who can only speculate about them.

A harmful marriage can be just as hazardous to your health as a harmful divorce. But a *specific* marriage and a *specific* divorce can result in a fulfilling life: it's up to each individual, with support from society, to make that happen.

Adult Children of Divorce Can Learn from Their Parents' Divorce Instead of Repeating It

Melvin Belli's heartfelt reflections on what he had learned *not* to do in his own series of divorces led to his conclusion about how to constructively nurture his own children after he was divorced. He recognized the harmful effects that a divorce based on vengeance directed against his ex-spouse had on his children, and that once he was able to change his attitude and behavior his children could flourish.

All divorced parents have a profound impact on the way their children see their situation in life. That does not mean, however, that children of divorce are straitjacketed into experiencing a lifetime of believing and acting as victims of a hostile, negative parental divorce, forever blaming their parents for the painful life they may be leading. Nor does it mean that parents who indeed practice a creative divorce (one in which the best interest of the children is always the major concern of the parents; where they don't use their children as weapons to hurt and harm each other by telling their children how "bad" their ex-spouse is) will inevitably generate healthy and happy adult children of divorce.

The way one's parents handle their divorce does not guarantee failure or success in one's life (neither is there such a guarantee, positive or negative, with respect to children who grew up in "intact" nondivorced families). Instead, there are tendencies that can be overcome or taken advantage of, rather than parental imprints that "must" damage a person for life or make him or her a success. All human beings are given two gifts of life: the gift of free will and the gift of resilience. The great writer Sean O'Casey was once asked what is the meaning of life. His reply was that life was simply an invitation to live. How one lives one's life depends on the choices he or she makes (free will) and the ability to respond skillfully to the challenges of adversity (that is the capacity for *resilience*, which the *American Heritage Dictionary of the English Language* defines as "the ability to recover quickly from illness, change, or misfortune"). Every individual on this earth has the capacity to respond to illness, change, or misfortune as disasters from which there are no escapes or as challenges to prevail over (to *prevail* means to triumph over adversities rather than wallow in them).

One objective of the following chapters is to share with you the experiences of the many different kinds of children of divorce who have led successful lives in the face of the traumas their divorced parents have inflicted on themselves and on their children. Their experience as prevailers over misfortune can offer you guidelines as to how you yourself can overcome similar difficulties.

In this chapter, we have itemized many different types of dysfunctional divorces. They can be viewed by the children of such divorces as either disasters that will inevitably damage their lives forever *or* as challenges that can be overcome in a successful way.

The Challenges to Prevail over Your Parents' Divorce

Here are examples of how many of the adult children of divorce saw their parents' divorce as a challenge to improve upon the past rather than repeat it.

• **The After-the-Wedding-Ceremony Divorce** becomes the challenge for an ACD to learn as much as possible about the personality and characteristics of the projected partner *before* marriage to resolve the differences that may be dividing the two of you. Informed choice takes the place of ignorance that led to the chronic pain of one's parents' marriage.

• **The Alienation Divorce** becomes the challenge to never take one's partner for granted, to learn that marriage is a journey of change and self-renewal that can become a lifetime of shared happiness and triumphs over misfortunes.

• **The "I Am King (or Queen) of the Castle" Divorce** becomes the challenge to identify what is the most important thing about married life—the cultivation of intimacy, not money. Intimacy has nothing to do with the feeling of "I'm more important than you are because I make more money." It has everything to do with two people respecting each other as equals, working together as a team, and valuing each other as the most important person in one's life. Without intimacy in his or her life, a person can be wealthy yet may be living in emotional poverty.

• **The Power-Struggle Divorce** becomes the challenge to acknowledge that saints are for heaven, not on earth. We are all fallible human beings and when we replace self-righteousness with compassion and forgiveness we can eliminate the power struggle from our lives.

• **The Injustice-Collecting Divorce** is the challenge to never become the mind reader of your partner in a relationship. If you mind read, you will be wrong most of the time. When you check out verbally and ask what your partner is really thinking or feeling, you will give yourself the opportunity to resolve problems rather than perpetuate them.

• **The Family-Triangle Divorce** becomes the challenge to establish an adult relationship with one's partner by setting limits to allowing your parents' demands to override your relationship to your spouse. Loving one's parents and one's spouse then becomes a cooperative enterprise, not a competition.

• **The Sexual-Betrayal Divorce** is the challenge to understand that mutual trust in each other is the foundation of a successful relationship and that nothing undermines this more than extramarital affairs. If one desires extramarital affairs, then there is no need for marriage, because mistrust was the way one's parents shattered their relationship.

• **The Bisexual Divorce** becomes the challenge to acknowledge toleration for behavior that may not be heterosexual. If you are heterosexual you need not condemn homosexual or bisexual behavior but recognize them as variations of the human condition rather than as sins. Should your own children become homosexual or bisexual there will not be any reason to love them less for who they are.

• **The "My Career Comes First" Divorce** becomes the challenge not to overemphasize the importance of one's career and career achievements at the expense of the balance needed to create a happy relationship. That balance needs to incorporate attention to the quality of one's relationship with one's partner—the need to incorporate respect, kindness, and compassion and his or her welfare and personal growth.

• **The "My Future Is My Past" Divorce** becomes the challenge to eliminate the belief you are valued solely for the money you make, and that you are a personal failure if you have not made the money you dreamed you "should" have made. The bottom line in life is not how much money you make but how successful you are in cultivating your relationship with your partner and your children. It is also the challenge to view your aging as an opportunity to grow and change for the better, rather than as an end-of-the-line catastrophe.

• **The Drug-Addiction Divorce** becomes the challenge to either eliminate using drugs entirely from your life or to use a very moderate amount of alcohol at the most. Because a genetic tendency is inherent in drug and alcohol addiction, it will be best to avoid them entirely if this predisposition is present in your family. Drug addiction is an attempt, in many instances, to heal the chronic pain in a dysfunctional relationship. In that case, the cure for drug addiction is to prevent it from occurring by creating a happy relationship.

• **The "I Never Wanted Children" Divorce** becomes the challenge to recognize that nothing lasts forever. Feelings and beliefs can and do change over a lifetime: what one man desires in his twenties may seem absurd or irrelevant in his thirties or forties. If a spouse never wanted children and then has them, this can become an opportunity to accept and love those children once they are born.

• **The "My Hobby Is My Spouse" Divorce** becomes the challenge to always remember that your spouse is the number-one person in your life. If you substitute the love of a thing (like a computer) for the person you marry, it can shipwreck your relationship. Counseling is the answer if you see that shipwreck developing.

• **The "Sex Is Everything" Divorce** becomes the challenge to put sex in its proper perspective in a relationship. Sex is an affirmation of a successful relationship. Otherwise it becomes a substitute for such a relationship. It is a gratuitous act in a successful relationship, not an obligation or a demand. It is also more than intercourse. It is the entire spectrum of caring and concern and mutual respect of two people; it is the coming together as a couple to help each other overcome the difficulties in their life and to renew their courage. When two people act in this way, expression of the sexual drive is a result of the concern, caring, and kind regard two people have for each other. Sexual intercourse, without this kind of intimate connection, is little else than an alternate form of masturbation.

The utilization of free will—the reality that life consists primarily of choices we can make, rather than inevitabilities we cannot influence—and the resilience all men and women possess to prevail over adversity can enable children of divorce to become healthy winners. However, to make that happen, up-to-date, truthful knowledge must be gained to refute the pseudoscientific charge that divorce "must" harm children for life. Our next chapter consists of this new, empowering knowledge.

2

New Hope

Research Findings Now Reinforce Positive
Self-Images for Children of Divorce

In spite of the conventional wisdom that predominates when
the issue of divorce and its effect on children is raised in the
media and by pseudoscientific professionals, a healthy dose of
reality is beginning to appear on this subject. As if to confirm
this fact while we are writing this chapter, an outstanding new,
solidly scientific study of the long-term effects of divorce on children that validates our own research has just been published.
Titled *For Better or for Worse: Divorce Reconsidered*, this most
comprehensive technical study of divorce in America involves
examining 1,400 divorced families and 2,500 children over the
last thirty years. It consists of the findings of author Dr. E. Mavis
Hetherington, psychology professor emeritus of the University
of Virginia, one of the best authorities on divorce in the United
States. The conclusion of her detailed research is that "the path-
way out of divorce need not be a prescribed path of dissolution,
but one of healing and ultimate fulfillment."

The most prominent gloom-and-doom findings about divorce
and its alleged lifetime negative effects on children have been the
work of Judith Wallerstein. Over the past decade, her three books

(*Surviving the Breakup*, *Second Chances*, and *The Unexpected Legacy of Divorce*) have been touted in the media as the definitive studies about children of divorce. They have been very influential because they seem to be based on "scientific" research. Her research has been taken for granted as convincing precisely because it has never been subjected to careful analyses in the media. The millions who read *Time* or watch programs like "The Oprah Show" have not been put on notice that her "research" is absurdly lacking in validity. In contrast to Dr. Hetherington's careful research, Dr. Wallerstein's findings involved only sixty families! Dr. Wallerstein's former associate Joan Kelly (who is the founder of the Northern California Mediation Center and coauthor of *Surviving the Breakup*) published an article in *Family Conciliation Court Review* stating Wallerstein's work is "full of conclusions that are scientifically invalid, ignore contradictory research, and unrelentingly emphasize the negative." This statement by Dr. Kelly appeared in the article "But What About the Kids?" in the May 1994 issue of *California Lawyer*. Mel was quoted in that same article which said, "Krantzler wrote that children are better equipped to weather a divorce in their families than most parents believe. . . . 'Wallerstein,' Krantzler says, 'helps people feel like victims and blame the divorce when they are unhappy. This thinking encourages a complete copout of personal responsibility.'"

We felt as strongly then as we do now about the negative effect of Dr. Wallerstein's books and media appearances on children of divorce and their parents. In our counseling practice at our Creative Divorce, Love & Marriage Counseling Center we have heard many teenage children of divorce, who saw us with their concerned parents, use their parents' divorce as an excuse for their dysfunctional behavior (e.g., bad grades, cutting classes, using drugs). They would say to us, in effect, "What can you expect;

it's all the fault of my parents' divorce; that's what the lady doctor on TV [or the radio] said divorce does to children."

The "lady doctor" they used as their justification was usually
Dr. Wallerstein. And because very few people read legal or conciliation journals, while millions read *Time, Newsweek,* and
women's magazines like *Redbook* and *Ladies Home Journal,* the
truth about children of divorce gets drowned in Wallerstein-like
distortions that become accepted as conventional wisdom.

Consequently, it is enormously gratifying to see a truly scientific work like *For Better or for Worse: Divorce Reconsidered* receive
some national attention because it can considerably help those
divorced parents who think that Wallerstein's "evidence" proves
their children will be damaged for life to recognize that such a
finding is fallacious. Dr. Hetherington's book can reassure
teenage and adult children of divorce that they need not believe
they will lead a lifetime of disaster because of their parents'
divorce. This new knowledge will enhance their self-esteem and
their ability to make positive things happen in their lives.

Four years prior to the publication of *For Better or for Worse:
Divorce Reconsidered,* a book appeared that also countered
Wallerstein's very pessimistic approach to children of divorce. It
was titled *The Nurture Assumption,* a research work written by
Judith Rich Harris. It is a more modest work than Dr. Hetherington's book and deals, in addition, with matters other than
divorce, but it is well-researched. She stated unequivocally "Her
(Dr. Wallerstein) books sold a lot of copies but as science they
were useless. . . . There was no control group of intact or self-
sufficient families with which to compare the children of her
patients and no way to filter out her professional biases. . . . Most
children of divorce do fine in the long run. . . ."

These two recommended books are particularly helpful to the
men and women who are impressed with statistics and with writ-

ers who have a "doctor" attached to their name. They all too often can convince themselves that what a doctor says statistically must certainly be true. However, some "doctors" are more capable and accurate than others—and statistics can lie and distort instead of revealing the truth. For this reason, the books by Dr. Hetherington and Judith Rich Harris are beacons of light in the field of divorce surveys where so much distortion exists.

The Myth of the Permanent Effect of the First Three Years

The widely circulated belief that children only develop to their maximum capacity in the first three years of their life is indeed a myth. Parents can relax and need not feel guilty for damaging their children permanently if they have lived in an unsatisfactory marriage or are divorced. An important new book titled, *The Myth of the First Three Years: A New Understanding of Early Brain Development and Lifelong Learning,* by John T. Bruer is a careful scientific evaluation of the repeated generalization that a child is damaged for life if he or she is not exposed to the best reading materials, the best music, or the best toys that exist. Of course these are the goodies that only parents in the top 10 percent income bracket can afford. All this can lead to is the creation of millions of guilty parents. Bruer assures parents such guilt is unnecessary. He demonstrates that people can grow and change for the better throughout an entire lifetime, rather than become trapped in low expectations of themselves because they never listened to Mozart in their first three years of life. Consequently, the psychological legacy divorced parents can leave their children is the enhancement of their self-esteem and reinforcement of their ability to prevail over painful experiences. In turn, these children of divorce develop the capacity to lead successful lives.

Another new book by excellent authorities reconfirms Bruer's findings. It is *The Scientist in the Crib: Minds, Brains, and How Children Learn*, by Alison Copnick, Andrew H. Meltzoff, and Patricia Kuhl. They state uncategorically, "The new scientific research doesn't say that parents should provide special enriching experiences in everyday life. It does suggest, though, that a radically deprived environment could cause damage."

This means the average well-intentioned parents who do the best they can (and are always on the alert to know how to parent better) provide children with the nourishment needed for their competent development. This is quite different from "a radically deprived" environment that can and does impair the appropriate development of children. Divorce in and of itself is *not* a radically deprived environment. It is how couples handle their divorce and how they nurture their children after a divorce that will determine whether or not children will be damaged by their parents. A creative divorce can (and does!) become an enriching experience for the children when the marriage itself was an intolerable battleground of abuse.

New Discoveries About Multiple Intelligences

Intelligence has been defined in the past as what one accomplishes on intelligence test scores and school grades. One's capacity to achieve in the world of work and be successful in interpersonal relationships was measured by how high or low these scores and grades were.

The research of Dr. Howard Gardner, Professor of Education at Harvard University, has proved this approach to be false. His book, *Frames of Mind: The Theory of Multiple Intelligence,* identified six types of intelligence which he listed as Linguistic Intelligence, Musical Intelligence, Logical-Mathematical Intelligence, Spatial Intelligence, Bodily-Kinesthetic Intelligence, and The Personal Intelligences.

Professor Gardner emphasizes that "We are all so different largely because we all have different combinations of intelligence. If we recognize this, I think we will have at least a better chance of dealing appropriately with the many problems that we face in the world."

This finding that each person is unique, with different combinations of intelligence, shatters the myth (which is still prevalent) that adult children of divorce are "defective" or "less intelligent" because some of them may have poor school grades and below-average intelligence test scores. These grades and scores are usually the consequences of the initial family disruption caused by divorce and the lack of any safety-net support (such as skilled child care, schools that teach rather than just caretake, and an end to poverty that makes one focus on sheer survival rather than high test scores).

In fact, as subsequent chapters demonstrate, very many ACDs are highly proficient in their practice of Professor Gardner's "Personal Intelligences." Gardner defines those intelligences as, "access to one's own feeling life—one's range of affects and emotions: the capacity instantly to effect discriminations among these feelings and, eventually, to label them, to enmesh them in symbolic codes, to draw upon them as a means of understanding and guiding one's behavior.

"The other personal intelligence turns outward, to other individuals. The core capacity here is the ability to notice and make distinctions among other individuals and, in particular, among their moods, motivations, and intentions."

Throughout the pages of this book, we present many examples of ACDs acting in precisely the manner that Professor Gardner identifies above as Personal Intelligences. In fact, ACDs had lived through their parents' traumatic marriages that ended in divorce (the types itemized in Chapter 1) and were able, *by using their personal intelligences*, to improve upon their parents' lives rather than replicate them. In our adult children of divorce research groups, we repeatedly heard one reply when we asked what was the starting point of their becoming achievers rather than clones of their parents. It was: "I learned early to separate out their problems from mine—I was determined never to repeat when I grew up what I saw them do to themselves."

They receive an A+ in Personal Intelligence. It is encouraging to note that the concept of multiple intelligences is now beginning to receive national attention and acceptance of its validity. Every popular book now advertised as a treatise on "emotional intelligence" is testament to Howard Gardner's original research. It is to be hoped that the more Professor Gardner's concept of multiple intelligences is accepted as reality, the more it will eliminate the stereotype of the less-than-normal adult children of divorce from our society.

New Divorce Role Models

In this new millennium, more and more well-known personalities are emerging as positive role models for adult children of divorce and the parents or surrogates who raised them. The enormously popular actor Leonardo DiCaprio is an adult child of divorce whose mother and father *both* provided the nurturing he needed to achieve his goals. The well-known actors and writers Matt Damon and Ben Affleck also have acknowledged they are adult children of divorce and that the way their parents have related to them enabled them to achieve success instead of failure in their lives. The celebrity impact of these stars enhances the image of children of divorce.

Perhaps the best known celebrity who frankly acknowledges his divorce and his total dedication to becoming the best father he possibly can be to his young son is Mark McGwire. In 1999, as the first man to hit seventy home runs, he proved he was one of the outstanding players of all time. But who can forget the time when he proudly waved to the ballpark audience, with his young son close to him, with pride in his being a father. As a divorced father, he spoke out to millions of men and women about his obligations as a parent and role model in an interview in *USA Weekend* on April 25, 1999. He stated, "I cherish my son and people should cherish their children more than anything in the world. . . . There's a lot of single fathers out there who don't pay attention to their children. Here's a single father who is in the limelight but is including his son. If I can do it, they sure could do it."

Mr. McGwire is very frank about the fact that he has had counseling to help resolve his divorce difficulties. As he said, "Relationships, it's like the toughest thing to do in the world, but nobody wants to talk about it." But McGwire is talking about it and telling people that going to a counselor is one of the best things a divorced parent could do for him- or herself and the children. These children of divorce, in turn, receive the benefit of the results of such counseling and can grow up secure in their knowledge that their parents acted in their best interest after their divorce.

New examples of the positive achievements of adult children of divorce are beginning to emerge in the national media at the very time we are writing this chapter. On July 2, 2002, an extensive article in our local newspaper, the *San Francisco Chronicle*, consisted of an interview with three twenty-nine-year-old African-American doctors who achieved their careers in spite of growing up in appalling poverty-stricken, drug-infested neighborhoods in New Jersey. All three were children of divorce whose parents split before they were in their teens (one was only two years old). They could have become what many of their peers became—drug addicts, robbers, or long-term prison inmates (one of these doctors said his father had been in prison so often that he thought prison was simply an apartment where he lived). Yet all three of these young men triumphed over adversity rather than becoming just three additional victims.

What made the difference? The answer is their resilience. They refused to be brainwashed into believing that they were doomed to lead lives of desperation and despair because of the environment in which they lived. Their formula for overcoming that environment was what one of them called his "three Ds"—determination, discipline, and dedication. Even though they had few, if any, positive neighborhood role models to guide them, they sought out others. One of the doctor's mother and father were both heroin addicts; he had a grandmother who became his source of encouragement. All three found powerful role models who reinforced their thrust to educate themselves to become the positive persons that they now are. One of them had a mother who told him higher education was an escape from poverty; another had a specialist in student development as a positive reinforcer who assisted him on getting financial aid and counseling; and another had a third-grade teacher who nurtured him like a mother and expanded his horizons. All three doctors needed a hand up (not a hand out) to succeed. They all make a point of praising the many people who have generously given their time, effort, money, and counseling support to help them succeed.

They acknowledge that no man or woman can succeed alone. It was their friendship from their high school days that reinforced their determination to succeed. Indeed it is their friendship and mutual support that resulted in the writing of their book called *The Pact: Three Young Men Make a Promise and Fulfill a Dream.* It has become a bestseller and focused national media attention on their dramatic story. Television interviews, movie rights, radio interviews, and articles in newspapers and magazines have all drawn attention to their achievements.

Indeed, one of the most important achievements these three doctors have accomplished is to help shatter the myth that adult children of divorce "must" become sad victims because they experienced life in "broken" households. Their story can encourage millions of other ACDs—black or white, male or female— to seek and find new horizons for themselves.

When parents adopt this approach to their own divorce, it can reinforce the capacity of their children to become achievers in life rather than victims.

Nontraditional: The Families of the Twenty-First Century

Children of divorce continue to be mislabeled as failures from "broken home" families. It is still too frequently assumed that divorced families are the exception to the rule that our culture still consists primarily of "intact" families (called *traditional families*) whose children are presumed to be healthier and happier than children of divorce. Our next chapter deals with the psychological fallacies surrounding this concept of "the intact family." As a preliminary to the next chapter, it is necessary to divest oneself of the myth that divorced families and children of divorce are dysfunctional exceptions to the rule, and that traditional families (defined as never-divorced families with two children, a wage-earner father, and a stay-at-home mother) are the norm in our society. The cultivation of this myth continues to have a devastating effect on children of divorce—a myth they are imprinted with in their earliest years and can persist throughout adulthood. Believing in this myth gives rise to unnecessary guilt, because many tend to romanticize that such a traditional family always was and is living eternally happy, while children of divorce feel they are confronted with a very mixed bag of life experiences. A child of divorce will feel like a second-class citizen, as an outsider, unworthy of being regarded as the equal of children from "traditional" families, if he or she accepts this imprinting. Therefore, it is necessary to dispose of the illusion that there is a superior force in our culture, an imaginary "traditional" family majority that creates happy lives, while children of divorce must lead stunted lives. When children of divorce believe this fantasy, they tend to unconsciously limit their own capacity to lead successful lives based on a healthy respect for their own competencies.

Throughout a major part of the last century, a certain truth existed in the belief that the "traditional family" was the norm rather than the exception until cultural changes that took place in the 1960s eroded that fact. The most popular TV family shows in these earlier years were "Father Knows Best" and "Ozzie and Harriet," which exalted the father who earned all the money, the mother who stayed at home to care for her husband and the children, who were all conforming, spanking-clean, drug-free members of a happy family bound together for life. . . .

But flash-forward to today's times. The 1950s-type family started to change when divorce became common in the 1970s, so that today one-half of all marriages end in divorce affecting one million children annually. The University of Chicago's National Opinion Research Center released a survey in November 1999 that revealed that so-called "intact traditional families" are a minority rather than the majority they once were. Only about 25 percent of households today consist of a never-divorced couple with two or more children living at home (down from 50 percent in the 1970s). Only slightly more than 50 percent of men and women are married today, compared with 75 percent in the 1970s. Sixty-seven percent of the people surveyed disagreed that parents should stay together for the sake of the children.

Tom Smith, the man who headed this survey, calls these changes "the modern family." In the modern family people no longer say that everyone should belong to a "traditional" family. Instead, it's up to adult men and women themselves to determine what kind of family they might have, including living-together arrangements and the right to remain single. Social approval no longer depends solely on being married once and forever with two children. A tolerance of different approaches to relationships is now a priority of today's times.

The challenge, therefore, is to find successful ways to make these new family arrangements work. As Tom Smith reports, "It appears that none of the trends will reverse in the foreseeable future and that most will continue."

Consequently, we can expect divorced men and women and adult children of divorce to become mainstream characteristics of American life in this twenty-first century. This can be an opportunity to improve the quality of people living those lives, rather than a Chicken Little sign that the sky is falling. Because the so-called "intact family" was never really that "intact" or problem-free after all, as the next chapter demonstrates.

3

The Myth of
the "Intact" Family

In our extensive research over the past three decades, we have explored the experiences of the men and women who grew up in "intact" families to determine whether or not they were living in much happier circumstances than children of divorce, as conventional wisdom would have it. Their answers surprised us by how often they said that they had fervently wished their parents would divorce, because living together was a continually painful experience for them. Here are some of the typical comments they shared with us:

• "It was so horrible when I was a kid growing up with an alcoholic father and mother," says John, age thirty-seven. "A day never went by without their screaming and throwing things at each other in a drunken rage and then they would beat me up. I kept praying they would divorce and leave me alone. No such luck, they stayed together until dad died of a liver so diseased it was the marvel of the hospital. I was seventeen then, and Mom got a grip on herself once Dad died. She went to AA and has been dry for the past twenty years. But I sure wish that would have happened when I was a kid."

- "My dad sexually abused me from the time I was eight until I was sixteen," says Anna, age thirty-one. "My mom stood by and denied it ever happened. What a marriage! I ran away at sixteen, supported myself, and put myself through college. I'm a high school counselor today, helping many troubled teenagers who have experienced sexual abuse like I did. God, it's so prevalent."

- "My father used to use my mother as a punching bag," says Brian, age forty-eight, "because she was uppity and didn't obey him. I used to hear her scream and how she would beg him to stop, while I shivered in my upstairs room. I remember having fantasies of killing my father when I was ten. When I heard mom's screams I would imagine I had a long sharp knife and I would stab him to death so he would stop pounding my mom. The violence only ended when my father got a stroke when I was thirteen. But Mom was so beaten down all she became after the stroke was his caretaker. They're both dead now—Dad seven years ago, Mom three years ago."

- "I'm gay. It's no big deal, just a fact of my life, just like being heterosexual is simply another fact," says Gary, age twenty-eight. "But my parents made it a big deal, moaning over and over about what a terrible punishment God inflicted on them to have such a wicked son. In fact, they kicked me out of the house when I was sixteen. Luckily, I had an uncle Harry who was compassionate. He and his wife, Jan, took me in and made sure I wasn't discriminated against. My parents still haven't accepted me. Only if I 'repent' and turn heterosexual will they consider me their son. I believe gender is genetically based, so to ask me to change is like asking a politician to remain honest."

- "We lived in poverty and it tore my parents apart even though they remained married until both died twenty years ago," says Carl, age fifty-four. "My father had no skills and was fre-

quently unemployed. Even when he worked, his wages were piti-
ful because the jobs were unskilled labor. Sheer survival was their
concern, not love for each other or for my brother and me—we
had to go to work when we were thirteen. Yes, I'm a stockbroker today, but I still shudder over the way my poor mother and
father lived and because of the way they had to live, I never felt
loved as a kid."

• "My father was a gambler," says Erica, age thirty-four. "He
used to drive my mother crazy: One week we would see lots of
money, the next we would be poor as church mice. We could
never plan ahead. He refused to go to Gamblers Anonymous to
break the habit and my mother felt she had to stick by him
because she thought it would harm my two brothers, my sister,
or myself if she divorced him. I would see her cry in the evening
when she was sitting at the kitchen table alone while my father
was out to the next casino. I wished my mom would divorce my
dad because I couldn't stand to see her weeping so often. I left
home when I was seventeen; I was lucky to get a college scholarship in a city far away from my hometown, which is just where
I wanted to be—far, far away."

• "My father was one big pain in the ass," says Mark, age
thirty-four. "He was always saying to me, 'It's for your own
good,' when what he really meant was that it was for his good.
For instance, when I played in Little League games he was always
arguing with the umpire when I struck out—which was often.
It's as if he was playing the game, not me, and that was so embar-
rassing to me. And when I said I didn't want to go to law school
like he did, he blew a fuse. Always trying to control me. I never
remember him asking what career I wanted to have. He assumed
I would become a corporation lawyer like him. My mother was
a wimp who always supported my father. She was afraid to con-

tradict him even though I knew she sometimes sympathized with me, but she never said so. Well, my brother became the lawyer and I became a newspaper reporter. Dad still thinks that's way below the level of being a lawyer. He doesn't know I think more of used car salesmen than I do of lawyers."

• "Mom used to tell me it was all my fault that her life was so miserable," says Mary, age thirty-six. "I can remember as far back as when I was eleven when I first heard her say that, but she was probably putting that trip on me even earlier. She kept telling me that if she hadn't been pregnant with me she would have gone to college, would have had a career, and gotten out of her unhappy marriage with my father. I had to suffer through her negativity toward me until I escaped to college. I had terribly low self-esteem because of my mother's bitchiness, and it took me years of therapy to realize it was her fault, not mine, that *her* life was so painful."

• "I always felt abandoned as a kid," Bob, age forty-nine, says. "Ever since I was seven my parents would lock me in the house from Friday night through Sunday night while they went out to party. It was a ritual with them every weekend—they both were heavy users of cocaine, and they had a sort of club with self-centered people like themselves in it. I would live in terror whenever Friday arrived, knowing they would leave me home with little in the house to eat. I not only wished they would divorce, but I also wished they would send me off for adoption to some kind family that would care for kids. No way. Even now I still feel uncomfortable if I'm alone at night."

• "I was an only child—it's better to say I was a lonely child," remembered Justin, age thirty-five. "My father was an electronic engineer who made a lot of money from his inventions. My mother didn't have to work, she had plenty of help in our large New York eastside apartment where we lived while I was growing up. Mother was self-absorbed and spent most of her time worrying about her looks and her clothes, and Dad was always working at his inventions. They made me feel like I was an imposition, rather than a son who was loved. They used to go on big vacations twice a year to far-off places, leaving me at the private school or with a nanny. I don't remember when the three of us ever went on a vacation together. Instead, they gave me all the toys I wanted—mini cameras and photographic equipment— which I loved. Expensive stuff, so they could say, 'Look at what we give you. How fortunate you are. Lots of poorer kids would sacrifice an arm and a leg to get the goodies you have.' Yeah, I know that old saying about being rich and being poor, and that rich is better. Of course, it was better for me to eat well, have good clothes, the best medical care, and an expensive school upbringing than to be poor. But I know that you can have all these things and be miserable at the same time. My family may have had money but no compassion. All they cared about were things— they had to have the best of everything. For them, it was most important to brag about the far-off places they visited that no one else they knew ever went to. Of course, they had to have the most expensive talked-about cars and would brag about their art collection. But as a kid all I wanted was their attention and love, which would have cost them nothing. And that's what I got, nothing. I may have been the rich kid in the neighborhood, but I was really poverty-stricken when it came to getting my parents' love."

When we asked these men and women would it have been better or worse for them if their parents divorced rather than stayed together, their answers were not the typical ones you might expect. Conventional wisdom would have it that at all costs it would always be better to stay together for the sake of the children no matter how flawed family life might be.

But not one of these men or women shared this belief. Divorce may have been tough to experience, they told us, but infinitely better than to live, as John did, in perpetual fear of family violence. Or Anna, terrified over being sexually abused by her father. Or Brian, fantasizing about stabbing his father to death because of his father repeatedly assaulting his mother. Or Gary, being excommunicated from his "intact" family home because he is gay. Or Carl, living in a fear-ridden, grinding poverty family where finding the next meal was the most his parents expected out of life. Or Erica, faced with a gambling-addicted father and a weeping mother who engendered a black cloud of despair over family life. Or Mark, who had to fight continually against being branded a clone of his father. Or Mary, who had to pay the price for her mother's bitterness over her lack of a career and her unhappy marriage. Or Bob, still experiencing abandonment feelings many years after his terrifying childhood. Or Justin, who lived in an emotional desert during his childhood.

The Power of the Individual

The examples we have shared with you could be multiplied many times over, because they are not exceptional in family life today. To call such families "intact" simply because parents have not divorced is to falsify the meaning of that term. The dictionary defines the word *intact* as "not impaired in any way." Yet each of the families noted previously were impaired in many ways.

Does this mean that "intact" families are better for children than divorced families or vice versa? Of course not. It all depends on the *individual* family, "intact" or divorced. Marriage and divorce are simply structures to be used for better or worse by the men and women who use them. In the examples cited previously, marriage was unskillfully used by couples, usually well-meaning, to create a great deal of misery in their children. This does not mean marriage will not enhance children's lives. Indeed, marriage, when practiced creatively, is certainly more desirable than divorce. When that occurs, there is no need to divorce.

Divorce, on the other hand, can also be creative in place of a self-destructive marriage. A vengeance-free, fair divorce that focuses on the best interests of the children is a far better atmosphere for children to grow up in than a marriage torn apart with self-centeredness, bitterness, and mistrust.

It is of primary importance to never underestimate the resilience of children. That Chinese saying, "Out of the mud grow the lotus" is applicable to each of the examples cited in the previous chapter. You might think that these men and women were damaged for life because all of them experienced very dysfunctional childhoods. Yet nothing could be farther from the truth! Here is what they told us about their present lives.

• John is a happily married man with two teenage daughters and says, "I learned early on to seek out counseling help for my family problems. That was the best thing that ever happened to me. I don't drink because I found out there was a genetic tendency in my family to be an alcoholic. I learned alcoholism was a disease, not a sign of personal failure. My poor parents didn't know this, unfortunately."

• Anna blocked out memories of her sexual abuse for many years. But eight yeas ago they broke through her denial of them and she joined a therapeutic group consisting of sexually abused women like herself. "That experience," she told us, "led me into my career of helping disturbed children. I still find it difficult to trust men, but I'm dating someone now who's helping me learn to trust again."

• Brian is married with three grown children. "I learned never to hit my kids and also to treat my wife as an equal partner, not like my mother. We have our problems, but nothing like what I experienced growing up."

• Gary is active in gay organizations that fight discrimination based on gender differences. He also is a magazine writer for a gay publication. He is outspoken and nonapologetic but says, "I do regret, however, that my relationship with my parents never got better, but I always hope it will mellow out some time in the future."

• Carl is unmarried but became a successful stockbroker. "I've never lost my fear of being poor like my parents were. That's what pushed me into being concerned about making money and probably why I'm successful at it. But right now I'm ready for something more. I'm dating a real nice woman and am thinking about getting married. Making money is not enough to fully satisfy me anymore."

• Erica was recently married. She is a successful stock market trader. "It's funny," she told us, "that I should be in a profession so close to gambling, like my father's addiction. But there's a big, big difference. I, myself, don't gamble in the stock market. It's just that I'm good with figures and management, so I get paid good money for what I do. I like the excitement and buzz of activity at work that makes the job so interesting."

• Mark believes he made the right decision in becoming a reporter in spite of his father's disapproval. "Dad is now giving me some grudging respect since he saw a recent series of mine on drugs and children earn a citation for excellence. But he still is under the delusion that lawyers are next to God. I've chosen not to marry, but that doesn't mean I never will. It's just that it's not my time yet. I'll know later when it is."

• Mary is now a designer of websites and loving her work. "I've gotten lots of praise for my designs and that makes me feel good," she says. "I used to be apologetic when I was praised for what I did. It was like my mother standing behind me telling me not to believe it because I'm no good and would never amount to anything. That's gone now, Mom is no longer standing behind me. I'm dating now and can accept compliments when a man says I'm attractive. That's a big change, since Mom made me feel I was ugly. It looks like I'm a late bloomer, but better late than never."

• Bob became a CPA, very well known for the competency of his work. "I'm better with figures than people," he says. "At least I'm in charge; the figures don't talk back to me like my parents did. They're safer to deal with. I've never been a cocaine user like my parents, but I've been an alcoholic. I've stopped recently and am going to AA. I've been divorced three times and don't think I'll ever marry again. I've no children because I never wanted them to experience the horror I went through as a kid. I'm happy enough, I suppose, but there's a hell of a lot of room for improvement."

• Justin's parents died in a plane crash a dozen years ago and left him with an ample trust fund for life. "It's a mixed blessing," he told the group. "On the one hand it's good never to have to worry about money. But it also undermined my will to achieve anything on my own. The money's an excuse for just drifting through my life. Until recently, that is. I'm now in therapy and it's been a tremendous help to me. It's revived my earlier interest in photography and I'm now putting in a lot of effort to become a good photographer. I'm learning from the best teachers. Marriage? Still scared of it. I would never want to have a child experience what I did."

The Promise in the Pain

If there is one thing we have learned in our counseling practice, it's not to generalize or stereotype people. Each person is an individual in his or her own right and has the capacity to overcome adversity, providing he or she has the will to do so and the guidance to move in new and more positive directions.

For example, on the basis of the dysfunctional family lives of the men and women who have shared their childhood experiences with us in this chapter, you might expect each of them to lead absolutely miserable lives once they grew up into adulthood. But each of them refused to become victims of their past. They saw promise in their pain: the promise to overcome the adversities of their childhood. And they had the motivation and determination to do so.

In the examples we have noted, it can be said that all of these men and women are still in development. All are still flawed in one way or another and need to work on those flaws if they choose to do so. They can't complain if they don't choose, because to achieve a good life means taking personal responsibility to make that good life happen. After all, saints are for heaven; here on earth all of us are fallible human beings. But we have the free will to make better choices if we wish to do so.

We have seen in this chapter when biased authorities voiced the alleged virtues of the "intact" family to disparage children of divorce, they have really built a fairy-tale castle in place of a structure based on reality. There are "intact" families that are fine places for children to grow and achieve, as well as "intact" families that are dysfunctional places that stunt children's growth. The same can be said of divorced parents' households. To generalize, however, is to lead the millions of men and women who are seeking help to improve their lives into a blind alley. An "intact" family is *not necessarily* better than a divorced household. Nor is a divorced household any better than a married household. It all depends on individual situations and circumstances. To generalize is to stereotype—and to stereotype men and women is to deny their individuality and their free will, which sparks their capacity to change their lives for the better. If the disparagers of divorce and children of divorce would have their way, they would make puppets, rather than individuals, of them all. They would deprive them of free will or the personal power each and every human being possesses to prevail over life's difficulties rather than drown in them.

4

The Myth of
the Absent Father

The media's repeated use of the terms "absent father" and "deadbeat dad" are brainwashing labels that can diminish the self-esteem of children of divorce. Children's parents are their primary and most important role models in life. Consequently, when the media perpetuate the false stereotype that most divorced fathers are generally uncaring, mean, selfish individuals (which these labels imply) who are intent on harming their own children once a divorce occurs, the children can be imprinted to believe that because they are the offspring of such fathers, they may be "worthless" also. Such negative labeling can have a profound effect and may inhibit children from moving positively beyond their parents' divorce.

Contrary to conventional wisdom, the "absent" father is the exception rather than the rule. We see this fact validated almost daily in our divorce counseling practice. We have seen "strong" men, ages anywhere from thirty to fifty-five, weep when they tell us how they desperately wish to see their children frequently after their divorce and are inhibited from doing so by the courts, by negative custody arrangements, and by vindictive spouses who use denial of visitation rights as a way of continuing to punish their ex-spouse long after the legal divorce occurs. Divorced mothers also experience this form of victimization, which should be avoided at all costs.

Divorced fathers are programmed by our culture to feel unwelcome as the continually caring, involved parent that many want to be acknowledged as being. Too often, mothers are assumed and regarded as the only loving parent of their children: "Our" children turns into "my" children. The mother then becomes identified as a "single" parent. The father, by this definition, is defined as being "absent." But is he really absent, so that Mom is a "single" parent, meaning she parents alone?

In our divorce groups the men who have children are usually vehement on this issue:

"Me, an absent father? No way!" says Larry, a forty-five-year-old man with three young daughters. "My ex-wife is no 'single' parent. She wasn't a virgin when we married and she didn't have virgin births with our three kids. Whenever she talks to me about the kids, she's always saying 'my children' this, and 'my children' that, as if I'm just a spousal support paycheck and nothing else. She's also bought the baloney she's a 'single' parent, and I have to fight every time just to see my kids regularly."

Whenever a divorced father in any of our groups objects to the use of the "single parent" label, loud voices of approval from the rest of the men follow.

The passionate resistance divorced men have about the "single parent" label is an indication of how far men have traveled in our society in desiring to be regarded as permanent, active, ever-present fathers to their children after a divorce. There was a time, not too many decades ago, when divorced men were considered to be irrelevant to their children's lives once the marriage ended. It was presumed they were a paycheck and nothing else: their children's physical, emotional, and intellectual growth was to be attended to solely by the mother. This seemed "normal" in those times, because a father's function in a marriage was presumed to be the sole family breadwinner and nothing more; raising the children was delegated to the homebound mother. In divorce, Mel was part of that generation and he can remember that his sole function at the time each of his two daughters was born was to wait outside the delivery room and then hand out cigars at the time of the birth. A standard routine of those times.

Today, scientific validation maintains that keeping the continuity of a child's relationship with *both* parents after a divorce is essential to the physical and emotional growth of the children. And this knowledge has filtered into the minds and hearts of most divorced fathers, who indeed dearly love their children and now have empowered themselves to voice this reality in their demand for equal parenting rights in a divorce. They no longer feel inhibited in voicing this demand through organizations such as the American Coalition for Fathers and Children, which are active in trying to make the courts and legislatures validate its reality.

Because many adult children of divorce grew up in households whose fathers held the attitudes that it was demeaning and "feminine" to exhibit their heartfelt nurturing capacity directly to their children, they may still believe they were "unloved" by their fathers. During gender-biased times, it was thought that men showing emotional love to their children was "wrong" and would betray a homosexual tendency. Mel has frequently counseled such adult children of divorce by sharing his own culturally conditioned background with them. He explains how he clearly loved his two young daughters but felt he had to hide his emotions and demonstrate his love for them only in terms of his material contribution to the family. He felt in that benighted time that a man like him could only show his love to his children by being a stable, employed wage earner, a man who provided them with all the material things necessary in life, such as decent housing, food, clothing, television sets, autos, and a college education. The emotional nurturing of the children was thought to be the sole province of the mother. Mel used to hear the statement then (a few decades ago!) that fathers were only considered useful in family life as "money-making machines."

This personal experience has resonated in many of the adult children of divorce we counsel. Frequently, they will reach out to an estranged father and will be surprised and happy that they had misperceptions of each other's motives and behavior that could be corrected, even decades later. Quite a number of fathers, in turn, may tell them that they had felt a permanent sense of loss of connection to them, sadly believing they were irrelevant to their children after the divorce—and they will eagerly respond to a second-chance, adult-to-adult positive relationship with their children by voicing their love for them.

Of course, there is always the risk of disappointment when such a reaching out for a reconnection and reconciliation occurs. And that does happen. But the risk of that happening is well worth the taking, because forgiveness for acting unskillfully in the past can enable a divorced parent and child (no matter how old) to enrich their lives through a reconciliation. If the reconciliation does not take place, one's sense of self is still enriched by reaching out.

Words That Wound and Distort Relationships

The old saying that "sticks and stones may break my bones, but names will never harm me" is false. In fact, words can not only hurt, but they can even kill: racist words, homophobic words, and words used to define divorce relationships can cause enormous harm. Consequently, it's important for everyone, divorced or otherwise, to recognize the extent to which the terminology used to define divorced parents and their children on TV, radio, books and articles, and on the Internet poisons our view of them and demeans their self-images. Recognizing the persuasive use of these labels is the first step toward eliminating them from our consciousness, which then helps divorced fathers empower themselves to assume their rightful place in their children's lives.

Let's analyze the Pandora's box of the typical phrases the media love to use to describe the divorced.

Divorced Parents

Wait a minute, just who are the persons getting a divorce? This label gives the impression that the *children* are getting divorced, not the two adults. Small wonder that young children, worried, ask their parents, "Are you and Mom/Dad divorcing me?" Children are very literal, and this simple label can become words of terror in their minds.

Absent Father

We have already noted the pejorative nature of this phrase. It presumes that when a divorce occurs, a father disappears of his own free will because he wants to have nothing to do with his children anymore. To speak bluntly, this label is pure slander. Our counseling experience and research reveal that a father's "absence," if it indeed happens, is not freely chosen by him. It is usually a result of an unfair court order or by vengeful attempts by his ex-spouse to bar him from meeting regularly with his children, even when the courts entitle him to do so. An unfortunate typical example of this "get even" action was shared with us recently by Jerry, a thirty-six-year-old man with a twelve-year-old son and a nine-year-old daughter:

It broke my heart. I had waited all year to take my kids on a month's vacation, as the judge's order said I could. I bought the plane tickets to Disneyland and my own ticket because my ex lives in St. Louis and I live in Chicago. So what happens? A day before I'm ready to leave Chicago, my wife sends me an E-mail saying Terri—that's my daughter—and my son, John, both came down with chicken pox and couldn't go with me. Naturally, if that were true, even though I would be terribly disappointed, I could understand their need to be cured, rather than go with me. But I later found out my ex had lied to me, just to prevent me from being with them. Sure, Terri did have chicken pox but was no longer contagious and John never had it. They both could have gone with me. Instead they got brainwashed by my ex that I didn't want to go with them because I was too busy at my work!

Jerry's face was a mixture of pain and fury, and his eyes teared as he recalled his missed opportunity to be with his children. Yes, he was an "absent father"—but absent by manipulation rather than desire on his part.

Vengeance is a gender-free attitude. Both men and women have an equal opportunity to hurt each other in a divorce because it is inevitably a traumatic experience. How couples handle that trauma and their willingness to set aside their hostility toward each other to act in the best interest of their children will determine the legacy they leave their children after the divorce. In Jerry's divorce, the legacy was one of hurting their children more than their parents. It is inappropriate to defend or negate all women in their reaction to their spouse in a divorce as it would be to defend or negate all men. Divorce offers equal-opportunity situations to hurt an ex-husband or ex-wife. It is imperative that the temptation to hurt and harm be destroyed if a divorced couple and their children are to lead a better life after the divorce.

As long as divorced couples continue to play the game of "getting even" with their ex-spouse in this manner, the children will be the ultimate victims. There is, however, an encouraging new tendency among both divorced men and women to understand the need to act in the best interest of their children, which means ending the "getting even" game. For in that game everyone gets hurt, rather than "even."

Custodial or Noncustodial Parent

As Alan, a thirty-one-year-old divorced father of a five-year-old boy, told us, "I looked up the word *custodian* in the dictionary. And you know what it said a custodian is—it's a 'janitor.' I'm no janitor and my kid is no piece of garbage. And then I looked up the meaning of *custody* and the dictionary said it meant being held by the police. It's like my child has committed a crime so that my ex or myself have to guard over him as a criminal. That's crazy!" Crazy and damaging it is. These labels serve no other purpose than to degrade parenting in a divorce and sets the stage for using the children as "custodial" or "noncustodial" pawns once a divorce is initiated.

Visitation Rights

When we ask divorced men how they feel about this term as identifying their relationship with their children, it creates an uproar of indignation. Alan, a forty-two-year-old man with two teenage sons, sums up their general attitude: *Visitation rights* is a B.S. term," he said. "No one has the right to call me a 'visitor' when I see my kids. I'm their father, *not* a 'visitor.' She got pregnant by me and I'm damn proud of that, because I wanted children and I love them. It is just another example of how fathers are put down once we're in a divorce."

It's a small wonder that many divorced men who dearly love their children feel like second-class citizens and Mel wasn't different in his own divorce. It was only when he began to question the truth of the labels mentioned above that they stopped having a control over his thinking of himself as unworthy. For all of these labels imply that *all* marriages are good and *all* divorces bad, without making the necessary distinction that there are bad marriages as well as good ones, and good divorces as well as bad ones.

Self-Empowering Labels in Place of Demeaning Ones

In our research with groups of divorced men who are concerned fathers, we have demonstrated how they feel about those labels that brainwash them into believing they must be of less value and worth to their children than their mother. When we asked them how we should change those labels into more constructive, dignified expressions of relationships between divorced spouses and their children once separate households have been established, here is the consensus of their suggestions.

Instead of a "divorced parent," they suggested the use of a "divorced couple with children" as being less confusing. At least it would send the signal to their children that only the *adults* are divorcing each other and that they are not divorcing the children. The fact that both parents will always love their children after the divorce is the education the children need.

Regarding "single parent," the divorced men and women in our groups were unanimously opposed to this label. Most frequently mentioned were three substitute labels, because the women as well as the men agreed that *both* parents were equally important to their children:

- "Coparenting relationship" was first, because it emphasized the *equal* importance of mother and father in nurturing their children.
- "Shared parenting" had a good sound to many of the men, who also felt their children would like that label.
- "Time-sharing arrangement" was considered a marginally satisfactory substitute for "single parenting." But it had too much the aura of a "condo rental" rather than a parenting arrangement to be a first choice!

"Custodial rights" sounded to most of the men like a dentist's drill on an exposed nerve. "Equal parenting rights" received an enthusiastic welcome as a substitute. This new phrase implies that the father as well as the mother are actively involved on an equal basis in nurturing the physical, emotional, and intellectual development of their children. The children can then enjoy the positive benefits of both parents in their upbringing, even though these parents are now living in separate households and may even have other partners now.

"Visitation rights" had the effect on the ACDs like a rattlesnake bite. They felt that those two words and how they were implemented by the courts and their former spouses needed to be eliminated from the English language. They felt "visitation" implied that divorced parents were interlopers in their children's lives—a visitor rather than a father or mother. The consensus was that "parental rights" would be a better phrase because it is neutral and does not give the children the impression that their father or mother is a less-than-equal partner in their lives.

We don't want to give the impression that word changes are the answer to the difficult problems experienced by parents and children after a divorce. But they are a significant part of the answer.

It's been said if you repeat a lie often enough, people will believe it. The danger exists that the very people who are lied about—in this case divorced men and their children—will incorporate these lies in their own psyches. They then deceive themselves and could believe they are personally unworthy, like the terminology that assaults them implies. In turn, they transmit low self-esteem to their children, which, if not reversed, will remain with their children the rest of their adult lives. Therefore, refusing to become victimized in this fashion and fighting for their rightful place in their children's lives is the next step after the disposing of the negative terminology directed against fathers—and children—in divorced situations.

Perhaps the most outrageous brainwashing concept of all that demonizes divorced fathers is the endlessly repeated "deadbeat dad" slander branded on the foreheads of divorced men with children. Because it is so universally used, we will devote the next segment to analyzing what truth, if any, exists behind this label.

Deadbeat Dads: A Halloween Story

It's a very scary picture that the media present: "deadbeat dads" are in the majority. They are cruel, uncaring men who have no feelings about their children. They hate their ex-wives and wish to punish them for all of the harm they believe their wives inflicted on them in their marriage. Now that they are divorced, they are getting even with their wives by not paying them the child support they are legitimately entitled to even though they could afford to do so.

This "deadbeat dad" media invention demeans divorced male parents in their children's eyes. It paints a bleak picture of these parents as selfish men intent on destroying "traditional family values" and damaging their children for life.

However, reality tells a very different story:

Some men—also women—indeed refuse to pay the child support they are legally required to pay and can afford. This is usually done out of spite, a desire to get even for the alleged hurts their ex-spouse had inflicted on them by playing a vengeance game at their children's expense. The "I'll refuse to pay child support until you allow me my visitation rights to see the children" game. Or its variation: the "if you don't give me the child support payment, then I will refuse to allow you your legal visitation rights until you do so" game.

The media rarely take notice of "deadbeat moms." It is true that women who lose custody of their children are ordered to pay child support in the same proportions as men. Women also play the vengeance-against-their-ex-spouse game. However, these "deadbeat dad" (or "deadbeat mom") situations are the exception rather than the rule in divorce cases. In the overwhelming majority of cases, lapses in child support payments are consequences of widespread unemployment and the proliferation of temporary or part-time, low-paying jobs now endemic in our society.

According to the U.S. General Accounting Office, mothers who receive less child support than they are entitled usually report that the fathers are simply financially unable to pay, not

because they don't want to do so. These women are more understanding of their ex-spouse's economic difficulties.

When parents act in the best interest of their children in their
divorce, more than 90 percent of men with joint custody and
nearly 80 percent of those with cooperative visitation rights pay
the entire child support obligation on time.

The United States National Commission on Interstate Child
Support's research on nonpayment of child support revealed, "If
you preserve the child's relationship with both parents, you will
rarely have a problem with nonpayment. And the first step in
preserving that relationship is to enforce visitation rights." Today,
there is a greater willingness by both men and women to develop
such a relationship after a divorce.

The Weapon of Mass Distraction

"Deadbeat dad" is a fraudulent label that is a weapon of mass
distraction.

Children are at risk from homicide, the leading cause of death
among fifteen- to twenty-four-year-olds, and it does not differ-
entiate between children of divorce or "intact" families.

In the past twenty years, more than fifty thousand juveniles
were shot to death by other juveniles, close to the number of
American deaths in the Vietnam War. The bullets did not dif-
ferentiate between children of divorce and those from "intact"
families.

One out of four children in our country goes to bed hungry
every night. Poverty and starvation does not discriminate
between children of divorce and those from "intact" families.
Millions of the working poor are experiencing this impoverish-
ment that is being generated by our society, not by deadbeat
parents.

We have said that when you repeat "deadbeat dad" often enough, you may begin to believe it. In this context, we are reminded of the story of the man who looked at the blank white wall in his living room and felt it needed something. So he went to a paint store, bought a brush and some orange paint, and started to paint the white wall. He made four long horizontal orange lines on the wall. Then he stepped back to view his handiwork. His face became terror-stricken.

"Oh, my God, save me, save me!" he cried out. "There is a tiger in my house, ready to eat me up!" He continued to stare at those four horizontal lines as if he were immobilized. The terror mounted in him until he wrenched himself into running out of the room.

In other words, it's of vital importance to guard yourself against Halloween-like imaginary problems like the "deadbeat dad" issue (there are more than enough *real* problems in our lives to cope with). Consequently, as an adult child of divorce, you can empower yourself by recognizing that society, cultural conditioning, and media brainwashing are the major sources of maligning divorced dads by calling them "deadbeats." You have the right in our democracy to object to this falsehood and act in concert with others to end its damaging effects.

5

The Myth of
the Permanent Loser

Adult children of divorce are generally reluctant to identify themselves as such. Through painful experience, they have been judged as "damaged goods," "lost causes," or always the "losers in a field of winners." There is always the need to resist believing these falsehoods to be true.

A typical reaction was told by Jerry, a twenty-nine-year-old member of our ACD group, who related his dating difficulties. "I've learned to keep my mouth shut about the fact that my parents divorced when I was seven, even though I try to be up-front with any woman I date. It's the look on the face of the women when I say I've come from a divorced background. The wheels in their head start turning and their eyes glaze over; they don't have to say it, but they sure show it. It's like I'm untrustworthy, a loser, maybe also an alcoholic or a heroin addict or womanizer, so get lost."

There's a cultural lag here. Because it occurs in half of all marriages, divorce itself is no longer considered a disgrace and is more often regarded by today's society as a fact of American life, not as a product of original sin. However, adult children of divorce do not get this same consideration because men like Jerry still get stereotyped as damaged goods. Women are equally vulnerable to negative labeling. Ashley, an attractive thirty-one-year-old freelance writer in our group, nodded in agreement with Jerry and said, "Sometimes similar things happen to me. Maybe it's because I feel a little guilty and apologetic about coming from an alcoholic family background, even though I don't drink or take dope. But it's also the fact that a number of guys I dated automatically tabbed me as a flake or dope addict when I told them my parents divorced when I was five. So I keep my mouth shut about that if I want to have a good time and maybe get closer to the guy I go out with."

The "loser" label, of course, is not limited to involvement in the dating game. Once one is stereotyped as having a "defective" personality because of your "unfortunate upbringing," the negative impact of those demeaning labels impair one's relationships in society at large.

We can acknowledge that dreadful things have happened to some adult children of divorce and that the imprinting of such abuse might last a lifetime. The same, of course, can be said of adult children who were abused in "intact" families. However, it is simply not true that these kinds of victimized men and women are typical of adult children of divorce. The fact is, most ACDs are as well-adjusted—or as dysfunctional—as people whose parents never divorced.

Because of the cultural denigration of ACDs, they always need to fight against the kind of self-victimization Ashley mentioned. If conventional wisdom has it that you are indeed a "loser" if you are an ACD, and if that conventional wisdom predominates in our society, then the tendency exists for that disparagement to become self-disparagement. Our culture has a profound impact on our own self-image. It's no accident that television is primarily an advertising medium that tells us repeatedly that money, material goods, and career status in life are everything, so buy, buy, buy! No one is exempt from this cultural impact. This demeans our self-image to the level of each of us becoming a product, a puppet to be manipulated rather than a human being. ACDs are not only exposed to this general demeaning of people, but also have the additional burden of struggling to eliminate the stereotype of them as being somehow "defective" by virtue of their divorced family upbringing.

It is to their credit that increasing numbers of ACDs are successful in rejecting the stereotype and in validating themselves as decent, capable, and competent people. Many are in substantial ways better for having triumphed over their past adversities than many other men and women who have grown up in more "privileged" homes.

The Importance of Resilience

Our own research has identified resilience as the driving force that successful ACDs have utilized throughout the difficult times in their lives. There is a new research trend that reaffirms our own observations. The *New York Times* reported on this trend (January 2, 2000) as the emerging field of "post-traumatic growth," which is defined as "positive changes in self-perception, interpersonal relationships, and philosophy of life for people who have undergone significant trauma." (This is another way of defining resilience). When we read this news report to our ACD groups and asked for some reactions to it, two persons in particular had dramatic stories to tell about how they themselves have lived through what this report is now acknowledging. The first to speak up, Alan, a thirty-two-year-old married man who is the director of a job-search program, had this to say:

I grew up in a house where my parents didn't really love me or my sister. All they cared about was their position in life, their money, their parties, and their drinking. Dad was a Chicago stockbroker who died six years ago, and Mom was a socialite who died of a heart attack when I was twenty. You could call me a thirty-two-year-old orphan since my birthday was last week. They were divorced when I was five and my sister, Kyra, was nine. After one of their usual drunken battles, my mother kicked my father out of the house and filed for divorce two weeks later. That breakup was so painful that I completely blocked it out of my mind until years later. All I remember of that evening was that I thought Dad left the house voluntarily and then decided never to come back. After he left, I remember Mom saying to me and Kyra, "Let's look at TV. 'The Brady Bunch' is on." We did and then I went to bed—or so I thought that's what I did. It was only years later that Kyra told me that halfway through watching "The Brady Bunch," I ran upstairs into the bathroom and threw up all over myself. I really had known the terrible thing that was happening but blocked it out of my mind because it was too painful to remember. I desperately wanted Mom and Dad to love me like in "The Brady Bunch"; that's why I remembered it so vividly.

My parents spent three years in court arguing over the property and money each felt they were entitled to. So you can see I was soured on marriage—look at the role models I had! But I fell in love with Maria and took the risk. We married when we were both twenty-seven, and it turned out fine, much to my surprise. But when we turned twenty-nine, Maria said she wanted a child and thirty was a good time in life to have one. That shook our marriage to its roots. I thought of my own rotten childhood, so I told Maria "maybe later, now is not the right time." But I really meant "never" because of my fear of the harm parents can do to their children. Maria knew I wasn't being honest and forced the issue. That was when we came to see the two of you. Maria is the love of my life; it would have been unbearable to break up. I had to face my fears and discover I was not doomed to be like my father. After all, I was not an alcoholic like he was, and my values were totally different from his. (I am the director of a job search program for people living in poverty). I like to help people, not screw them.

My marriage was based on caring and love, rather than selfishness. In fact, my sister, Kyra, tells me how much she envies me and wishes she could have a marriage like mine. So I reluctantly agreed to have a child after all. But I must tell you, I was scared half to death when Maria became pregnant and had to fight the feeling that having a child would break up our marriage. How crazy that was! Because after Stephanie was born two years ago, it made our marriage tighter than before. And I found out I was a good parent—I went to all the training programs and after-birth groups for new parents and discovered I loved every minute of it. I'm actively involved in changing diapers, preparing meals, taking turns caring for her when she wakes up in the middle of the night, and playing with her. What a great experience! I can just see my father, wherever he might be, scratching his head, saying, "How could Alan go so right when I trained him to go wrong!"

The second person to tell how she, too, was "resilient" was Lisa, a forty-five-year-old woman whose parents were divorced when she was seventeen. No one in Lisa's family ever expected much of her—and Lisa lived up to that expectation. When she was growing up she was a fun-loving, attractive-looking child who was very sociable and enjoyed making people laugh. Her social life took precedence over her academic performance so her grades were always poor.

I was the class clown and liked it that way. My older sister was the brain. She was three years older than me, and I was expected to get the As and Bs my sister got. I was always "Penny's younger sister," not myself. So the only way I felt I could stand out was to be sociable and funny, the exact opposite of Penny. Penny got mostly As in school, while I was a B-minus student.

My parents took sides. I felt I was only appreciated for being able to make people laugh, but Penny was valued because she was the serious student. So my parents encouraged Penny to go to college and encouraged me instead to marry early and forget college. My parents got divorced when I was seventeen, so I had to go to work in an office because I was living with my mom and we had very little money. But that wasn't the only reason I didn't go to college. I also felt I couldn't cut it because Penny was so much smarter than me. That's what I thought, I had a very low self-image. But I don't believe it's true now.

On the other hand, I kept avoiding marriage as a "solution" to my problems. For me, my mom and dad were not very good role models. I was scared that I would repeat their divorce. So I kept on working and feeling rather empty, like something was lacking in my life. Not marriage or children particularly, but here I was in a nowhere office job on a modest salary. "Is this all there is to my life?" I kept asking myself when I turned thirty.

I didn't know it then, but that was the beginning of when I started to turn my life around. It was 1985 when there was a lot of talk about a woman becoming her own person and taking charge of her life. I heard of women starting their careers in their thirties after being housewives until then, and women even in their forties who were going to college for the very first time and getting a degree. Over the years I had read a lot. For a person who thought she wasn't intellectual, I still liked to read. But it was mostly limited to mystery stories and romantic novels. But because I liked to read—period—that has been my saving grace. So I decided, after hearing about all these women who were making something of their lives, to see if I could get through one college course. To test the waters, so to speak, I took the plunge and enrolled in a continuing education course at my community college on American women novelists. It was a revelation! So many talented women who wrote such wonderful books. Willa Cather became my favorite, with My Ántonia and Death Comes for the Archbishop *affecting me deeply.*

And, here I am fifteen years after taking that first course, with an M.A. in English literature. And I'm teaching at the same community college where I took my first course!

It could be I'm a slower learner when it comes to relationships. I've dated rather casually over the years. But whenever I started getting close to a man, I would break the relationship off. And even if it was the other way around and I was dumped by a guy, I would somehow feel relieved, like feeling I had a narrow escape. Escape from what? Escape from a marriage like my parents. But now I think I've broken that habit. It's dawned on me—maybe I am a slow learner!—that I don't have to reproduce my parents' marriage. Maybe I can create a good marriage by avoiding the lack of communication, the verbal abuse, and the affairs my dad had. At least now I'm willing to risk marriage. There's a man in my life that I'm very fond of. I'm going to try not to run away from him.

These examples of adult children of divorce resilience are not exceptional. We hear them all the time. It is high time our society recognizes this resilience and celebrates the achievement of ACDs.

The previous examples were all heterosexual, but in our experience homosexual adult children of divorce are even in greater need of validation. Our society is still split on deciding whether or not homosexuality is simply an alternative acceptable form of human behavior or something to be condemned. An emerging majority in our society believes in tolerance for all kinds of sexual behavior between adults so long as that behavior is mutually agreed upon and is not harmful to either party. We are both proud to be members of that emerging majority. A number of homosexuals (men and women) have been in our adult children of divorce research groups over the past two decades, and they are primarily outstanding individuals—kind, decent, caring, empathic, and achieving persons. Most of all, they are resilient in the face of outrageous discrimination because of their sexual orientation, as if being an ACD was not bad enough. An example of resilience of the most positive kind comes to our mind with the story of Jeffrey, a thirty-two-year-old openly gay man who is a CPA. Here is what he told the members of his ACD group:

When I was fourteen, my parents divorced and at the same time kicked me out of both of the new places they lived in. I was an only child and they knew I was gay because I showed evidence of being different from other boys since I was nine. Both of my parents were bitterly disappointed in me and even said that I was the cause of their divorce. I even believed that B.S. when they kicked me out as if I was garbage. It was an easy way to avoid their taking personal responsibility for the hell they created with each other, which started long before I was born. They didn't have me until they were married for ten years, and I learned later from my relatives that they were fighting with each other almost from the first day of their marriage. In fact my mother left home twice, and then came back before I was born.

I'm a quick learner, so it didn't take me too long before I felt I wasn't to blame for my parents divorce. They shoved me onto my aunt Sarah, who was happy to take me in, so I was lucky that I was kicked out! My aunt Sarah was an unmarried lady in her early fifties when I began living with her. She was very tolerant. She knew I was gay and it didn't matter at all to her. I've never felt I was "strange" because I was homosexual—homosexuality has always been just another form of human relationship. It's part of the human condition that goes back as far as Plato.

So whenever I hear people calling me "a sinner" or "wicked" I have to laugh, because in many ways I'm a very conventional guy. I have a good stable job. I'm an independent CPA and tax consultant. Yes, I have a lover. Gary and I have been domestic partners for seven years—and we're monogamous.

Our relationship is just like a good heterosexual one: we love each other and consider each other our own best friends. We believe monogamy is the only way to establish and maintain mutual trust. We want our relationship to last a lifetime and have even gone to relationship counselors when we have problems we can't personally solve. If people can't tolerate us it's their problem, not ours. We have nothing to apologize for, and we hope that eventually we can live in a society that accepts our sexual natures on a nonjudgmental basis. Progress is being made in that direction, but it's still too slow. But Gary

and I don't let anger get the best of us when we're discrimi-
nated against. We have a favorite saying that carries us
through those times. It's that living well is the best revenge.

There are more Jeffreys in this world than most people imagine—people who are tolerant, flexible, and nonjudgmental with
a firm sense of self-regard. They are sterling examples of
resilience. Resilience, in less fancy terminology, means if you are
stuck with a lemon you can make lemonade. It means you have
a choice—not an inevitability. You can either wallow in self-pity
and helplessness, or see ways in which you can triumph over your
difficulties. The adult children of divorce we have quoted saw
how they could better their lives even though tornadoes were
enveloping them. It is the way you see your situation that will
determine whether you will allow yourself to be victimized by
misfortune or triumphant over it.

6

The Myth of Fearing Long-Term Relationships or Marriage

In our counseling practice with men and women who have grown up in families that have never been divorced, we have observed much fear of commitment to a long-term relationship or marriage. Relationships are scary, they tell us; and as for marriage, look at their parents' lives—daily disasters. In terms of conventional wisdom, you would imagine they grew up in bitter divorced households rather than in "intact" families.

Dave—a thirty-eight-year-old, never-married man whose parents were in a loveless marriage but never divorced—is typical of many men and women who suffer from what we call the "virus of commitment anxiety" precisely because of the fear they might replicate the barren relationship their parents had. Dave has a cynical frame of mind, which is really a cover story, because underneath, he is a sensitive, caring person who wants closeness but fears it at the same time. His cynicism masks his vulnerability. When asked by his friends when he's going to get married, he answers, "I'm like Anton Chekhov, who said 'if you want to be lonely, be married.' That's just like my parents. They deserve two purple hearts for staying together."

The figures on the state of marriage today appear to validate Dave's commitment anxiety. The number of married men and women has dropped from 71 percent in 1970 to mid-50 percent today. Why try to engage in a committed relationship if it's bound to fail? After all, one out of every two marriages ends in divorce as the Census Bureau confirms. And if you were married once, you stand double the chance of getting divorced if you married again. (First marriages typically end after seven years, second marriages end after three or four years.)

For all too many men and women who have lived in households where Mom and Dad stayed together unhappily, the facts about marriage that we have cited are being used as excuses for avoiding any long-term commitment or marriage. They have taken for granted the family imprinting they received about staying together permanently ("Look at what it did to my mother and father"). They felt that marriage inevitably fosters a barren existence. They never questioned while they were growing up whether or not marriage meant only what they saw their parents living through, and they never reflected in their adulthood that better relationships could exist.

On the other hand, in our research with the many men and women participating in our adult children of divorce groups, we have found—what even surprised us both—a primarily upbeat view of long-term commitment and marriage. Not because they wanted to replicate their parents' relationship, but *in spite* of it. While growing up, the adult children of divorce (who are currently involved in successful long-term relationships) were able to disassociate themselves emotionally and intellectually from their parents' marital problems. They viewed themselves as observers, not as participants, of family wars. This enabled them to learn from their parents' disastrous relationship rather than repeat it. The quality they possessed was one of the forms of resilience (a topic we discussed in Chapter 5) that enabled them in their adulthood to become winners instead of losers in long-term relationships with or without a marriage license.

These ACDs have the ability to consider themselves as outsiders. It seemed to come naturally to them to view their parents' relationship problems as jigsaw puzzles, and that they had to seek out the missing pieces to make sense of those puzzles. And the crises they experienced, both before and after their parents' divorce, made them see their family situations as opportunities to rethink the meanings of commitment and marriage. Their outsider point of view enabled them to do so.

Avoiding the Twelve Minefields of Marriage

Over the past three decades, we have interviewed many hundreds of ACD men and women who are successful in their long-term relationships to find out what went right rather than wrong to enable them to be continually optimistic about their situation. We first asked what they felt went wrong in their parents' relationship. Twelve "minefields of marriage" were repeatedly voiced by the adult children of divorce in our ongoing surveys on the most significant dangers in their parents' marriages that they themselves recognized and avoided in their own relationships. We are itemizing these destroyers of any potential for long-term happiness with typical comments from members of our ACD research groups.

Avoid Marrying Too Early in Life

Adult children of divorce more often marry later in life than the men and women who grew up in nondivorced households. They typically tell us that their parents married in their late teens or early twenties, and that they didn't have a clue as to what went into a good relationship or how to raise kids. ACDs were determined to avoid this trap. Marrying in their late twenties or early thirties was their norm.

Avoid Choosing Marriage to Escape from Problems

ACD parents had convinced themselves that marriage would solve their personal problems. Instead, it only created greater problems for themselves and the children they later had. They had suffered drug or alcohol addiction, physical abuse, neglect, incest, loneliness, anxiety, or insecurity in their own lives and thought that marriage would be their ticket to happiness. Most of them never went to counseling or sought other forms of help once they did marry. They had only taken the problems that plagued them prior to their marriage into their new relationships. And instead of leaving them behind, their partner also had problems of his or her own that they too thought marriage would solve. So more unresolved problems were created after they married than prior to making that decision.

Avoid the Poison of Blame-Making

ACDs typically experienced a form of marital warfare known as blame-making as they were growing up. Their parents were continually blaming each other for their problems, rather than focusing on how they could solve a problem that was causing difficulty. "Even if one of my parents forgot to bring home a carton of milk, that would be enough to trigger off an argument that would never seem to end," one ACD told us to the universal acknowledgment of the rest of the ACDs in her group.

Avoid Complaint-Collecting

"My parents made me feel I was living in a courtroom instead of a house," said Ellen, a thirty-five-year-old ACD group member. "They always had a list of complaints directed against me. It could be as small as coming home five minutes late from a friend's house, or 'why did you get one B instead of all As on your report card.' In my house, the cup was always half empty, it never was half full. I never once heard my father give my mother a compliment, like when she wore a pretty dress or cooked an especially great meal. And I always heard my mother complain to my father about his not making enough money. So their complaining about me was to be expected, I suppose." We heard similar reflections repeatedly from both the men and women in our research groups. These memories were branded into their souls.

Avoid Drugs or Alcohol

The use of drugs and/or alcohol were endemic among the families of adult children of divorce while they were growing up. We've heard horrendous stories of childhood neglect, daily physical violence, and paychecks used for drugs or alcohol in place of paying for food, rent, or clothing. These parents never knew they were addicted and that it would take more than willpower to stop their use.

Because of having had to live in a drug- or alcohol-induced violent household, many adult children of divorce have made special efforts to learn as much as possible about these addictions and have tried to avoid them in their own lives. Many have found that they themselves tended to replicate their parents' addictions, but unlike them, they sought out help—such as attendance in AA—to eliminate the effect on their own lives. They frequently discovered that they may have inherited a genetic tendency to become addicted to alcohol, and, in that case, they were avoiding alcohol for the rest of their lives.

Avoid the Make-Me-Happy Relationship Infection

This is the belief that your partner exists to make you happy. Mark, age thirty-three, shared this reflection with the group. "My mother always expected my father to solve all of our family's problems. It was like she was always expecting my father to be her permanent entertainment industry. What a delusion! I have to laugh now, because my father expected the same requirement from her! So they were always on a collision course because they were feeling disappointed with each other."

Whenever a man or woman made a comment like this (or a very similar comment) we would hear some outright laughter emerge from the group that seemed to be saying, "none of that silliness for me!" Happiness in a marriage occurs when two persons are happy in themselves before they marry. Each person is responsible for his or her own happiness, but a good marriage has the synergistic effect of enhancing the happiness of each in their sharing the challenges of life together and prevailing over them as a couple.

Avoid Physical or Emotional Abuse in a Relationship

All of the adult children of divorce in our ongoing research groups acknowledged they experienced some form of emotional abuse in their families, even when their parents did not physically abuse them (although physical violence against them as children occurred in at least half of their upbringings). Feelings of being demeaned, isolated, lonely, and experiencing an onslaught of verbal abuse and unjust criticism were some of the emotional problems they had to deal with. And where alcoholism or drug abuse was rampant, they had the additional burden of physical abuse to contend with. The ones who were able to salvage their self-esteem did so by their ability to cultivate resilience. They sought out resources of enlightenment (e.g., counseling assistance, educational courses, or social work groups) that enabled them to transcend their family conditioning.

Avoid the Entitlement Illusion

"Each of my parents believed that life and their marriage 'entitled' them to good fortune. But what they taught me was that life entitles no one to anything, except being alive before you die." Carol, a thirty-one-year-old human resources manager, was speaking.

My parents never understood that. They didn't know they were asking for the impossible, that they had to make their own happiness—that and nothing else was what they or anyone else is entitled to. All I can remember growing up was their bitter resentments and angry confrontations and their name-calling. I always avoid using obscenities because every time I hear someone say one, it's like hearing my mother's and father's voices all over again.

I know now that those abusive words were expressions of their pain and disappointment with each other. They were their ways of saying, "I was unhappy when I married you, but I expected you to make me happy. And I'm bitter and angry that you failed me. You betrayed me!" Of course, no one was betrayed, except themselves.

No one in the ACD group in which this was spoken could argue with this point of view. The words they heard from their own parents' mouths had been either the same or variations.

Avoid the "I'd Rather Be Right Than Happy" Syndrome

If there was one aspect that all of the adult children of divorce in our groups could agree on that existed in their parents' lives, it was their mothers' and fathers' joint addiction to the "I'd rather be right than happy" syndrome. It always appeared more important to each of their parents to "win" a family argument than to compromise differences in a compassionate manner. A relationship then became an ongoing war of attrition of trust. Festering feelings of bitterness, injustice, and self-righteousness were remembered by the ACDs as one of the legacies of their parents' relationship. That legacy prevailed within their parents' marriage and became exacerbated in their divorce. In the divorce, each parent wanted the child or children to take his or her side, to "prove" mom or dad was "wrong" and a bad person. It was the resilience of these adult children of divorce that enabled them to refuse to take sides and focus attention instead on renewing their own lives.

These ACDs told us they hated the feeling of being "torn apart" by their parents during their bitter divorce. Each parent wanted to "use them"—in the words we heard frequently from them—as a "weapon" to hurt and harm the ex-spouse. Each parent would complain to his or her children that the divorce was the fault of the ex-spouse and that the children should realize that he or she was a mean, cruel, vicious, and insensitive person. No matter what age the children were at the time of the divorce, parents who held fast to this "I'd rather be right than happy" syndrome would inflict this burden on their children. They were saying to their children, in effect, "Choose me over your other parent as the good parent and agree with me that your other parent was a bad person."

The ACDs told us how confused they were over their parents' actions. "It was crazy-making," one of the ACDs told us. "My father would tell me how terrible my mother was, and vice versa. But I knew I was made from both of them. So when my father said my mother was bad that meant to me that one-half of who I was was bad. And when my mother said the same thing about my father, then I thought the other half of me must also be bad. So when they thought they were hurting each other, they really were hurting me most of all! Because, before I learned better, I felt for a time that I was no good, that my parents were bad so that made me bad!"

Avoid Sexual Affairs

Many of these adult children of divorce told us that their marriages or long-term relationships were successful because, among other things, they put great emphasis on monogamy. "It's the only way to build up trust in a relationship," said George, a forty-one-year-old happily married man. "Nothing destroyed my parents' marriage more than both my mother and father having affairs. It was like tit for tat. If my father was having an affair and Mom found out, then she would retaliate by having one also. It destroyed their marriage. Why get married at all if all you want to do is screw around? You can do that easily without getting married. But if you want love and trust—and I certainly did— then you choose monogamy. Not because you're forced to do so—it's my own personal choice. Because if you feel forced to do so only because your partner would want that in a marriage, then it's a no-win marriage. You'll screw around after the ceremony, believe me."

No one in any of our groups disagreed with this assessment.

In our extensive counseling work with couples where marital infidelity was the central issue, we frequently discovered that the infidelity was really a cry for help. It was not that the unfaithful partner did not love his or her spouse, but that certain critical needs he or she had were not fulfilled in the relationship (e.g., a need for far greater appreciation, a need for better sex, a need for greater intimacy, or a need for greater understanding and compassion). Often, the unfaithful husband or wife expected one's spouse to validate his or her personal worth. But the reality was that those needs were being sought for fulfillment in all the wrong places. In counseling, the unfaithful partner would discover that he or she was the cause of his or her own marital problem, not the partner. No one else could resolve the problem except oneself. For example, a man feeling insecure about his career might seek validation from a woman outside the marriage. And a woman might have an affair to prove that she is still attractive, because she fears turning forty. Problems of this kind are internal rather than external.

In these kinds of instances, we have been successful in helping couples renew their relationship, rather than get divorced, if enough love remained. However, rebuilding trust would always be a long and painful journey. Mutual trust means to regard each other as the number-one person to care more about you as a person than anyone else will, to express your vulnerability without being judged negatively; and to have a partner who will renew your courage instead of demean you. This is the reason for marrying. And nothing—but nothing—will erode that mutual trust other than extramarital affairs. As we have told many a couple,

"If you wanted to be married and also have affairs, forget about marriage. It's easier to hire a maid and wander through serial relationships. If you want intimacy, the trade-off in a good marriage is choosing monogamy—a choice to be made freely, rather than to be demanded—as the grounding for a lifetime of mutual trust."

Avoid the Togetherness Trap

"You must think, feel, and behave like I do. You must like what I like and do what I do—or else you don't love me." This is the togetherness trap that most ACDs' parents fell into.

It was one of the major reasons for the fights, anger, hostility, and name-calling that paved the road to their divorce: to insist on togetherness at all times is not love but a form of control that masquerades as love. It consists of a combination of pressures (e.g., "You must have sex when I want it." "You must agree with me about how to raise the kids." "You must like all my friends and my hobbies." "You must vote the way I do."). It is an attempt to force one's partner into a conformist mode. This is the result of possessing very low self-esteem. It is really a fear of believing oneself unlovable if one's partner has opinions of his or her own. Such an attitude misinterprets differences between a couple as rejection of one's sense of self. It's a fear-based attitude, not one based on love.

Avoid the Power-Play Game

This is the game that continued throughout many ACDs' parents' marriages and was a major cause of their divorce. The power play was the father's demand that their mother "toe the line" because he was the sole or major wage earner who regarded his wife's earnings, if she did work outside the home, as "pin money" or devalued her contributions to home and family because she was a stay-at-home mother. The equation was money equals power equals total control of the decision-making process. The spoken or implied demand in these ACD families was "because I'm the one who pays the bills, I have the right to expect total conformity to my wishes. There is no room for compromise; only my word counts."

The women's revolution alerted everyone to the unfairness of this kind of treatment. It was considered "normal" for the culture to exalt the wage earner at the expense of the stay-at-home mother. "Fairness" was not even considered to be an issue. Many ACDs' very early years were spent in families of this type. It was always an unfair arrangement, but until the culture itself began to change (after the 1960s) and that change validated the fact that women make an *equal* contribution to a marriage regardless of the money they earn, women stayed in that old-style marriage. When they began to demand equality and mutual respect, but their spouses refused to acknowledge this need, many divorces began to occur over a way of life that could no longer be tolerated by women.

However, even today we work with many couples who are divorcing where the man in the case will indignantly remark, "Why should I pay my wife any alimony? She's always had a free ride in our marriage. I was the only wage earner and all she did was stay home with the children!"

But when the divorce actually occurs and an ex-husband of this type begins to live alone, he is often shocked into a recognition that without the backup help of his wife at home, the children wouldn't be taken care of; the essentials of family life wouldn't be shopped for; the house would not be attended to;

and cleaning, laundry, and food preparation would all disappear from his life. If he had had to do all of these duties and obligations himself, he would never have had any time to fulfill his career goals.

The power-play game still persists in modern form today. Today, most families have two-career partners and, at times, the wife earns more than the husband. Here, the reverse power-play game can—and does—occur. The wife calls the shots, the husband feels demeaned. But a breakup need not occur as it did with the ACDs who experienced the earlier form of power play by their parents. In today's climate of opinion, a greater societal awareness of the need for fairness and equality in a marriage exists, and these qualities must be put into practice if a marriage is to be a happy one. Counseling today is an accepted way of resolving this kind of problem (it is beginning to be acknowledged that it is the strong person who goes to counseling to resolve marital problems, not the weak one—the weak one runs away from or denies the problem). When most older ACDs grew up in their family prior to a divorce, going to a counselor was considered a sign of personal weakness or a signal you were "crazy"!

The Eight Ways Adult Children of Divorce Create Positive Relationships

The adult children of divorce who have successful long-term relationships can attribute that reality to their taking personal responsibility to make positive things happen in their life. No cop-outs, no fault-finding in others to excuse one's own fears and inadequacies. Repeatedly we've heard statements like, "Growing up, I lived in a house that resembled a war zone rather than a family. So I had to make lemonade out of that lemon!" In other words they refused to play the role of victim that they saw one or usually both of their parents play out on a daily basis. Consequently, while it was important to discover what these ACDs avoided in their own relationships that their parents didn't avoid, it was equally necessary to explore and define the ways in which they took personal responsibility for making their long-term relationships work well.

Here is what ACDs report as helping them to build positive relationships:

Respecting Each Other as Separate Individuals

These ACDs were determined to value their partner as a separate individual and regard him or her with courtesy and decency, validating what he or she has to say about any issue even when not necessarily agreeing with a point of view that might differ from one's own. "My parents were pleasanter to an acquaintance, a salesperson, a fellow worker, or a friend than they were to each other. They used four-letter words just on each other, and I used to say that when I grew up I'd never be like that." This is the kind of statement we frequently heard.

Valuing Each Other's Differences Instead of Regarding Them as a Threat

They learned to appreciate each other's differences and showed each other the space and time to develop their own interests and abilities as well as what they had in common.

"We learn from each other," an ACD told us. "My wife has taught me to appreciate nature and earthy things because I grew up in the city streets of Chicago. As a city boy, I was even afraid of small dogs. Now I have two of them, two Maltese, and wouldn't think of living without them. On the other hand, because I'm more of an intellectual—not smarter than my wife, just different—I've been able to acquaint her with art museums, poetry, and foreign films, which she never was exposed to before. And she likes them very much. Our differences have added spice to our relationship, rather than poison like they did with my parents."

Making Relationships as Equal as Possible

Quite often, we heard observations similar to the following:

"In these times, my wife works a full day, just as I do, so it's only right that I share the housework with her. I make more money than she does, but she has an equal right to make important decisions with me. I didn't marry her because I could dominate her by making more money, I married her because I loved her, period. I wasn't hiring a maid who I could order around, like I saw my father do to my mother."

A common thread exists in all the ACDs we counseled, and that is this need to make a relationship as equal as possible if it is to succeed. They had witnessed the gross inequality, the eternal one-upmanship in their parents' marriage and saw these practices led to divorce. Of course, their parents were unaware that they were insensitive about the need to fulfill their partner's desire to be respected as an equal; to have their needs acknowledged as worthy of consideration would imply a willingness to compromise or accommodate where disagreements occur. However, dysfunctional families lack the awareness of how and when to cooperate with each other. They are like two ships passing in the night, misunderstanding each other until a time develops when their two ships collide into a divorce.

In these dysfunctional relationships, a husband and a wife are trapped into mistaking suggestions for improving the behavior of one's partner as criticisms and complaints instead. "You never hang up your clothes before we go to bed. Why do I have to do it for you all the time?" This is what a wife caught in this unequal relationship trap will say (we have heard this statement hundreds of times in our counseling practice). Similarly, a husband will say, "You're always spending too much money. You buy a dress and wear it once and never again. What do you think I am, made of money? Spend less on unnecessary things."

The tone in which these statements are made is usually tainted with anger and resentment. The bottom line is that both the husband and wife feel attacked, put down, and criticized as if each were a little child. It's as if Big Mamma or Big Daddy is laying down the law and you are being forced to comply with your partner's demand.

When this kind of communication occurs, the stage is set for each to believe his or her partner is being unfair and trying to impose an unequal relationship. The implied signal he or she hears is the sound of "I'm more important in this relationship than you are so you better toe my line." The demand for the husband to pick up his clothes is then mistaken by him as an attack on his person. And the statement the husband makes to spend less on inconsequential items is then interpreted as an accusation that she is a poor excuse for a wife.

The inevitable then happens. The husband responds by attacking his wife by changing the issue ("You never dust the table in the living room" may be his typical response). The wife will also change the issue and perhaps attack her husband's "filthy smoking habit, which you always say you will give up but don't!" when she hears her husband tell her she is an out-of-control spender.

They have not treated each other as equals, but as a person one must dominate to get one's needs met. It is only when they treat each other as equals—deserving to be listened to with respect—that a positive resolution of family concerns and disagreements can be accomplished. Here is the way that can happen:

- **Understand that the way in which you say something will determine whether or not your partner will even hear what you have to say.** In the previous example, both the husband and wife have legitimate issues that need to be respected and attended to. However, neither of them is dealing with the issues they present (e.g., the issue of sloppiness on the part of the husband and the spending habits of the wife). All they are responding to is the sound of each others voices: the harshness, the attack quality, the righteous indignation, and the judgmental criticism that are implicit in their communication with each other. Consequently, they feel they have no alternative but to attack back because they feel their positive sense of self is threatened. Arguments like this escalate to charges and countercharges and are exchanged until both the husband and wife are exhausted. Nothing has been solved, and resentment festers. They have not heard the content of what their partner wants to be discussed but are only hearing what they believe is criticism of their person. In other words, the way in which they talked to each other prevented their issues from even being heard!

- **To be heard, talk in a normal tone of voice, and point out you are not criticizing your partner but wish to draw his**

or her attention to an issue that concerns you. Your partner then will listen to the issue because he or she now knows you are not criticizing but are concerned about a problem he or she would like to discuss. Respect your partner as an equal when differences of opinion exist between the two of you. You will then be able to evaluate in a fair way the validity of your partner's concern. Even if you agree to disagree, do so respecting each other as having an equal right to his or her opinion. Above all, never attack your partner as a person. It's important to state you may disapprove of your partner's *behavior*, but do not disapprove of him as a human being. The danger phrases always to be avoided are: "You never . . ." and "You always . . ." These phrases are character attacks that seem to focus on behavior but really are heard as an attack on one's sense of self.

To summarize: It's not what you say to your partner that will get yourself heard, it's how you say it. In a good marriage *everything* is open for discussion and resolution when a husband and wife respect the way they talk to each other.

Cultivating the Power of Forgiveness

The belief in the need to practice forgiveness and to apologize to one's partner for any harm that is done was imprinted in all of the ACDs who have successful relationships. Here is the consensus of their thinking, which is the exact opposite of what their parents did while they were growing up.

Past hurts recalled, remembered slights and putdowns, cruel acts done in anger, harsh words that cut like a knife—these were "normal" events they saw their parents create while they were growing up. They later learned their parents weren't "bad" people but did hurtful and harmful things to each other not knowing how to avoid such actions. They never forgave themselves or each other or decided to take the next step of learning how to eliminate their destructive behavior so it wouldn't be repeated.

The ACDs who have successful relationships learned what *not* to do by observing their parents' angry behavior. For many of these ACDs forgiveness meant forgiving their parents for their hurtful behavior and using their power of forgiveness in their own relationships to successful effect.

Knowing the Difference Between Your Partner as a Person and His or Her Behavior

One of the way stations on the road to these ACDs' parents' divorce was their inability to understand or practice the message that their partner was *not* the behavior they disliked. When spouses repeatedly use unkind words to each other, brainwashing occurs as if it is directed against the person rather than the behavior that is disliked. The truth that you can hate some of a person's behavior but still love the person was unknown to the parents of today's ACDs. Consequently, each felt any criticism was an attack on their personhood. In the long run, instead of eliminating the behavior they disliked, they eliminated each other from their lives by getting divorced. The successful ACD learns from this defect in his or her parents' relationship and makes every attempt to avoid it from happening in their his or her relationship. He or she would be quick to say, for example, "Look, I love you, but I don't like the amount of money you spent on that computer gadget you just bought without consulting me." This focuses the issue on the problem to be solved, namely how much money should be spent, rather than labeling one's partner as a selfish person, which would sound like an attack against the person, leaving the issue of solving how to spend the family's income hanging in the air.

Seeking Outside Problem-Solving Help When Nothing Else Works

ACDs in successful relationships tell us they never hesitate to seek outside help from a marriage or relationship counselor when they are faced with what seems to be irreconcilable differences. They would tell us, "Our parents always believed it was a sign of personal failure if they would reveal to outsiders that they couldn't solve their marriage problems. So, they never solved these problems and got divorced. It's the strong person who goes to a counselor not a weak one. How dumb it would be if you had a heart attack and wouldn't go to a doctor because you thought you should fix your own problems. Well, it's no different if you believe you have a broken heart because things are going badly in your marriage. That's also dangerous, because it can cause depression which can make you physically ill. So it's only sensible to go to a counselor to give you some insight on how to resolve the problem you and your partner are facing—going together because you don't go to get divorced but instead to get rid of the behavior that's liable to cause you to divorce."

Confronting and Overcoming Any Unfinished Business Inherited from Childhood

Successful ACDS don't hesitate to seek out professional help with the problems in their interpersonal relationships when it is needed. However, there are many unresolved problems in all people's lives—problems from childhood—whether one grew up in divorced or nondivorced households. Many of the ACDs in our groups went to counselors before as well as after they were involved in a relationship and found that counseling was enormously helpful in resolving unfinished issues from the past that were still plaguing them in adult life.

For example, many successful ACDs were alcoholics in their earlier years, replicating their parents' addiction. They were appalled that they were repeating their parents' behavior when they had determined they would never do so. Instead of giving up and remaining alcoholic, they took personal responsibility to seek out professional help and to attend Alcoholics Anonymous sessions to break the habit. Once they had been told that they had an illness (alcoholism is usually based on a genetic predisposition) and it's not a sign of lack of willpower, they stopped drinking permanently.

They contended with other negative inheritances from their dysfunctional family backgrounds such as incest (not only girls by a father or a relative, but also boys had been attacked). Some discovered they had an Attention Deficit Disorder that had been left undiagnosed. Because an Attention Deficit Disorder (which is a chemical brain imbalance) can inhibit a person's functioning during an entire lifetime, help for this disorder was a paramount necessity. Recent national media publicity about this illness and the resources that can keep it under control have been utilized by many of these ACDs.

Another one of the major concerns ACDs had to contend with was attempting to resolve problems by violent means. Such men and women grew up seeing their parents physically abusing each other. It appeared they used violence against each other as a way to attempt to solve their marital difficulties even though this behavior intensified their problems. Consequently, a number of

ACDs grew up unconsciously believing such behavior between two people was "normal." When they discovered it was instead abnormal, they sought out and received professional help to eliminate this behavior from their lives because they had consciously decided years ago they would never act in this manner when they grew up. Once they were in touch with the unconscious programming that triggered them to replicate their parents' antisocial behavior, they were able to establish new, nonviolent methods to solve their problems.

Practicing Tolerance in Place of Judgmental Behavior

ACDs have an unacknowledged advantage over the men and women who grew up in nondivorced households: they are exposed to a far wider variety of lifestyles because once divorced, their parents moved in different directions, different neighborhoods, or cities; associated with different individuals; and became involved in new relationships.

When their parents lived together before divorcing, these ACDs usually had little exposure to our multicultural society. Many heard their parents voice negative statements about people of other ethnic groups, immigrants, homosexuals, the unemployed, and poor people in general.

The divorce gave many of these children a fast education in tolerance that otherwise might have taken them forever to learn. The same parent who bad-mouthed the unemployed and the poor could (and not too infrequently did) become one of that same put-down group. The area an ACD might live after their parents moved away from their old neighborhood might be mixed with people from various ethnicities and backgrounds. The ACDs found out that those "others" were good people with whom they could become friends. A parent might change his or her sexual preference from being attracted to a person of the opposite sex to one of the same gender—and the ACD may find that new lover of one's parent likeable and friendly. The word *gay* or *lesbian* no longer elicited fear and loathing in his or her mind. And if a parent remarried, the stepparent may be totally different from one's own parents in personality and behavior and a compassionate, generous person in his or her own right. "It takes all kinds of people to make up this world. I'm not God to pass judgment on them—but my parents did before they divorced, and all it got them was a divorce!" That about sums up the way many ACDs view the world.

7

How Adult Children of Divorce Become Good Parents

When asked, "Are you bringing up your children differently from the way you were brought up," ACDs who have children answer, as if in unison, "Very differently!" In fact, nothing elicits more passionate, lively, or thoughtful responses from ACDs than this question. Their own growing-up experiences were their guidelines on what to avoid with their own children. "We want to nourish our children, not scar them," was the thrust of their comments.

Contrary to conventional wisdom, the majority of adult children of divorce want children and a family life. Not the family life of their parents, but they know they have an alternative because they have the tools that their parents did not which will enable them to create a good life nourished by good relationships. In today's times, relationship and parenting counseling of high quality are available. And the Internet has many authoritative websites with resources and information that can assist anyone who has the will to seek them out. And that is precisely what these adult children of divorce possess—will.

In our groups, we always reserve time for discussions, questions, and feedback on how these adult children of divorce are raising their own children if they have any (or how they would like to raise their children if they are considering having them). They usually start by being very vocal about the negative ways they felt their own parents dealt with them. But, we then focus on how they do things differently with their own children. We ask them, "What are the components of good nurturing that you are giving your children? And how do those components differ from the way your parents related to you?" The viewpoints came from both men and women (we always tried to have equal numbers in our groups).

The list that follows contains those essential qualities they were attempting to practice and also instill in their own children.

- Positive role modeling
- Love cultivated through kindness and empathy
- Validation of all feelings
- Open available communication
- Gender equality
- Personal responsibility
- Building self-esteem

Although each group differed on the emphasis they placed on the various qualities they said were necessary for establishing a healthy relationship with their children, they always agreed that the combination of them indeed were required for creating secure and able children. Each ACD would remember the lack of some or all of these qualities as central to the painful development of their own childhood. They are acutely concerned about remedying that lack by trying to nurture them in their own children's psyches.

Through the personal life experiences of those ACDs, an understanding of these qualities had been hard earned. They were embodied in their own psyches only after they had painfully experienced their nonexistence in their own families of origin. Through either self-knowledge and/or psychological counseling, they arrived at their new value system. Each ACD had a different emphasis, a different feeling of deprivation, as they reflected back on their own childhood. Here are some of their stories.

Positive Role Modeling

All of the ACDs in our groups placed a universal emphasis on the need to practice this quality above all others with their children. David—a forty-one-year-old software engineer, who has been married fourteen years and had one daughter, Lindsay, age twelve, and a son Tom, age nine—eloquently summarized his feelings.

When I was a kid, I believed my parents were my entire world (I suppose everyone thinks that). I was always observing my parents—the way they talked and behaved toward each other and, most important of all, the way they dealt with me and my two brothers. To be blunt, they treated each other and us kids like dirt! Our family was always one paycheck ahead of becoming homeless. Looking back, I think my mom and dad were scaring each other, always worried about just existing. No joy, no happiness—only whether they could make it to the next week. So that was what we three kids grew up with: two role models who were showing us the world was a dangerous place, and that we shouldn't expect much of anything from it but danger and disappointment. Luckily, I had a role model outside of my family who saved me from re-creating my mother and father's environment.

He was my high school science teacher who was a kind and caring guy. He thought I had a talent for science and nurtured it. And he also nurtured my self-confidence, which was zero when I first went to high school. I learned from Mr. Jensen how important it was for a kid to have good adult role models—and that's exactly what I try to be to my own children.

All the ACDs affirmed the paramount importance of being positive role models to their children, and they were making a conscious effort to do so. They had different experiences from David, but their conclusion was the same as his.

What David said about parents being a child's whole world in his or her earliest years is very true. Because children are so helpless and vulnerable, they depend on their parents for their very survival. The early imprinting they receive tells them that the way their parents relate to each other—and to the children—is the way the world will relate to them and they to the world. Of course, later experiences modify the child's view and behavior. But often, at unconscious levels, the earliest behavior they viewed in their parents' household may predominantly influence their grown-up behavior. For example, the low self-esteem a child may experience in his early years may prevail into adulthood; the negative role-models of his or her parents may be perpetuated when he or she marries and passes on the put-downs they themselves experienced to their own children. Of course, this need not happen. But, it takes commitment to cope with these negatives and to overcome them with help from others, such as psychological counseling and positive mentors. It's up to each individual to seek out help when he or she discovers his or her life is in disarray.

The positive role modeling that these ACDs are determined to practice consists of incorporating as many of the following qualities as possible in the way in which they relate to their own children.

Love Cultivated Through Kindness and Empathy

Children not loving their parents is the exception, rather than the rule. In our ACD groups, we ask, "Do you believe your parents always loved you?" The answer, almost always, is "yes!" This was true no matter how traumatic the experiences many of these men and women were subjected to when they were living in their parents' household. George, who is a thirty-two-year-old ACD, affirmed this vividly when he stated, "Because my father abused me—I mean physically hit me in the stomach or my face—and because my mother had divorced him and died soon after (so I was living with my father) I was asked by the court to choose between living in a foster home or staying with my dad. He was an alcoholic, a roaring drunk at that time, but I didn't hesitate a moment. I chose living with my dad in spite of what he did to me. I wanted him to change, to be a better dad, and thought I could do it by staying with him. He was a kind father when he was sober, but I'd say that only happened maybe 20 percent of the time. Fortunately, he did get his act together by the time I was thirteen—he went into a rehab program and stopped drinking forever."

We would hear similar stories from many men and women who had been subjected to bitter abuse—physical or emotional abuse or even incest—who agreed with George. Yes, they loved their parents in spite of what they experienced. And—no matter how often they were disappointed—they always hoped their parents would change the way they related to them. This should not seem surprising. All human beings are made from their parents. Consequently, to leave them forever is like eliminating a part of themselves.

A great love gap often exists between children and their parents. Parents love their children in one way, while children yearn to have their parents love them in their own way, which may be very different. With adult children of divorce, this love gap was often a chasm in their own childhoods. Here is a typical example.

Mary, age twenty-seven, singled out the absence of kindness in her childhood—before and after her parents divorced when she was nine—as her giant love gap. Her parents were so involved in resenting and attacking each other while they lived together, and they were equally harsh toward Mary. After their divorce, it seemed to Mary that they continued being angry with each other. "It was," Mary said, "as if their divorce was a continuation of their empty marriage." It left Mary feeling as if she were an innocent observer of a train wreck. Consequently, she had always placed kindness as the top priority in establishing her own relationships. "Kindness," she says, "is the one thing that touches me most."

Mary believed her parents loved her but showed their love only in how she was physically cared for. But Mary wanted to be loved with direct expressions of kindness. She singled out this quality as the major element she was cultivating with her own children, so that they would not experience the love gap she had.

Validation of All Feelings

There are no such things as "good" or "bad" feelings: they are all present in every human being to be understood rather than judged. Yet, this is a fact of human existence frequently ignored by parents who are often well-intentioned but unaware of the harm that can come from judging or condemning the feelings expressed by their children. This is true of children living in non-divorced households as well as children of divorce. In our ACD groups, this issue seemed to be of paramount importance. Many of them had lived in very dysfunctional households prior to their parents' divorce where they mistakenly interpreted their parents expressions of feelings such as anger, hostility, resentments, and sadness as being "bad" and therefore to be avoided at all costs. As Gordon, age thirty-nine, put it:

I always felt such feelings were dangerous, because whenever my parents showed them they made me feel as if my world was coming apart. I remember as a kid of eight that the screaming and the yelling and the crying that happened so often with my parents made me think they were ready to put each other in the hospital and I would have no one to take care of me. So those feelings were very scary to me and I learned to suppress them in my own life. I always was sort of guarded and put on a happy face even when I was feeling miserable. It was like I wasn't showing who I really was whenever I dated women. The dates always turned into disasters. A good friend told me that maybe going to a counselor would help me, which I did and learned that it was OK to acknowledge all my feelings. So I am very alert to allowing my own kids (I'm married and have two boys and a girl) to express all their feelings. If they are angry or sad I try to find out what's bothering them, rather than saying these are bad feelings, that they "shouldn't" be angry or "shouldn't" feel sad. My counselor once told me that feelings are like seeds beneath the snow that are clues to telling me why I may be angry or sad and what I then can do about my situation.

Arnold, age thirty-seven, always wanted empathy from his parents. "But they were always so self-centered," he said. "It was as if my sister and I didn't count. My parents had money—you could call them very well off—so they had nannies and maids take care of us while they always went away on trips without us. What my sister, Nan, and I wanted was quality time with Mom and Dad, for them to understand our needs as well as theirs. But that never happened. I suppose that's why I'm attentive to what my own children need and want—I mean their emotional needs. Nan and I had plenty of material things, but they never made us feel happy. I believe that's why I make every effort to understand, not condemn, all of my kids' feelings."

Open Available Communication

Almost all the ACDs in our groups said they grew up in families where they felt they had to censor what they said to their parents.

Here's an example from Jim, age thirty-six:

My father wouldn't tolerate any disagreements with him. And my mother was always afraid to contradict him. What he said went, and he made no bones about it. If I disagreed with what he said, I could be put on restriction or he would put a strap to my behind. I never knew when he would think I was out of line, so I would keep my mouth shut when he was around. Looking back, that was awful, and I decided when I grew up and if I ever had kids of my own I would make sure to respect them and listen to anything they wanted to tell me. I have two boys—they're eight and ten—and I darn well make sure I find time to talk with them and make them feel free to tell me anything they want to without fearing I would punish them for saying something out of line. It's like I have a second chance for myself. My father never used to go out of his way, even an inch, to talk with me or respect my opinions. So when I make myself available to my own children and respect their opinions, it's like I'm telling my father, "You see, Dad, this is how I would have liked to be treated." He's dead now, but I would like to believe he's hearing this.

Nothing makes a child feel he or she is a person of value and worth—deserving to be cherished—more than parents respecting them in the way Jim explained he treats his own children.

It isn't only verbal communication between parents and children that needs to be attended to. In many instances, reading the nonverbal signals children give to their parents can often be more significant than words. Reading the body language of children (particularly when they are very young and are incapable of verbally identifying their feelings) is of paramount importance for a good parent-child relationship. Susan, age twenty-eight, told the group of her own experience with this issue.

There was so much screaming between my mother and father that went on years before they divorced, which was when I was seven. That scared me because whatever they screamed about was never resolved. It was over and over again—the same old things, about not enough money, about jealousy, about insensitivity, about in-laws. I was a silent observer. Oh, how I wished they would be quiet for a change. But that never happened. I was too young to identify that I was scared, and that I wanted to be reassured that my parents weren't going to become violent and hurt themselves and me physically (which they never did, it was always verbal abuse). I was always living on the edge. My parents were so busy fighting each other verbally that they paid absolutely no attention to my feelings. I had hoped and prayed Mom or Dad would come over to me and say something like, "Honey, you look so sad. What are you feeling?" Or, "Why are you so quiet? Would you like to say something to me?" Or, "I see you're all by yourself. Would you like to take a walk with me?"

But this never happened. So I grew up being a shy, timid follower, afraid to make waves or communicate my feelings directly. I was always the silent, wary observer—always wait-

ing for somebody else to begin a conversation or introduce themselves to me at a party. That is until I went into counseling when I was twenty-one and got some real insight into what had happened in my family. It was like finding the solution to a detective story. It was a whodunit, in which as a child, I thought my parents were arguing because I was a bad kid. I wanted to improve their relationship, but because I couldn't— they had to do it themselves—I thought I was a bad, rejected person. Only after counseling did I realize that my parents' arguments and divorce were their problems not mine. So, is it any wonder that I'm very attentive to the way my own kids (Mary is three and Barry is five) communicate with me non-verbally? I'm very quick to pay attention to their feelings and talk to them. It's a great way of communicating and I still ache for what I personally never had.

Attention is communication. Children in any household— "intact" or divorced—need this form of communication more than money or material distractions. Spending attentive time with your children is the most valuable "commodity" you can give them.

Gender Equality

The following example comes from Kimberly, age thirty-one:

My father treated my mother like she was a maid rather than as a wife who deserved to be treated as an equal. They divorced when I was eight and I lived with my mom until I was eighteen. My mom told me she couldn't stand it any more, being treated like she was worthless, since my father felt he was the only one entitled to make all the important decisions in our family. She said my father was a good provider and she never told me he was a bad person, but that he was stubborn. He had grown up in a family where his own father ruled the roost, so he had felt it was only natural for him to do the same.

My mom blossomed after the divorce. That was the time in the late seventies when women were becoming aware of their own power and felt that it was their perfect right to be treated as equals with men. I remember her being impressed by what Betty Friedan and Gloria Steinem were saying then. Mom, after her divorce, got a college degree in human resources and later became a personnel manager in a large furniture company. She became a great role model for me after her divorce—not before it! I also went to college and got a degree in foreign languages—I now teach Spanish and French. I'm looking forward to getting married. I'm living with a great guy. We want to have children and you can be sure I'm going to raise them as equals if I have any girls. And if I have only boys, I certainly will teach them to respect women and treat them as equals.

The women in our ACD groups were in agreement with Kimberly. Some of them had such an assertive mother as a role model even before a divorce; others had a mother who never became assertive, before or after a divorce. And some only grew into self-respect and self-reliance after a divorce. But all of these ACDs believed that teaching their own children about the need to practice gender equality was a necessity in raising children. A recent interest among these ACD women is their desire to maintain their femininity as well as being regarded as equals to men. They did not want to replicate men as their role models. They wanted to affirm their uniqueness as women along with their desire for gender equality. It is this approach that many of them now wanted to transmit to their own daughters.

Personal Responsibility

All of the men and women in our ACD groups affirmed that the most important value they wished to instill in their own children was that of personal responsibility. The ACDs themselves had learned from their own parents' divorce that they had to rely on their own efforts to make positive things happen in their lives after the major trauma of divorce. Some of them had parents who taught them personal responsibility. But other parents kept victimizing themselves by always blaming others for their post-divorce difficulties. As Gordon, age forty-five, said,

> *After the divorce, I lived with my mother, who kept crying and feeling sorry for herself all the time. She had good reason to be unhappy. My father had been a drug addict and blew all the money he earned on cocaine, so even before the divorce it was a stretch to pay the rent or have enough to eat. The household money went up my father's nose—he had used so much cocaine that it blew a hole in his septum. I never saw him again after the divorce. My mother's helplessness forced me to work my tail off and to grab as many jobs as I could. I was sixteen when the divorce happened and tall and strong as an ox, so I worked to bring the bread home helping stock groceries, being a helper on construction sites, and doing janitor work in sports stores.*
>
> *It made me feel good helping my mother out and helping myself by what I was doing. In fact, I became a role model for my mother! When she saw how much I was doing to improve our lot in life she started to change her own behavior and*

became resourceful in finding employment herself and in mak-ing new friends. It's a cruel world out there when you have no money and—let's face it—nobody gives a damn about you when you're broke. So the buck has to stop with myself. First of all, I tell my own two kids, you have to count on your own head and your own hands to make things happen. You need help from friends and organizations, if possible, but they can never substitute for your taking personal responsibility for the direction of your own life. I tell them they have to motivate themselves and then turn that motivation into deeds. I did that. I'm not bragging, but instead of saying "poor me," after my parents' divorce, I set the goal for myself to become an elec-trical engineer because that work always fascinated me and that's what I am today. My two boys, who are fifteen and sev-enteen, can be anything they want to be. Our society gives them that opportunity, but they have to take personal respon-sibility for that to happen. My father substituted drugs for per-sonal responsibility and destroyed his own life. I never forgot that, and that's why teaching my kids to become self reliant and self-motivating is so important to me.

By experiencing the negative example of parents' lack of such responsibility, like in Gordon's case, some ACDs learned the value of personal responsibility and the need to pass it on to their own children. Many others learned the importance of personal responsibility from their own divorced parents, who were good role models, because they showed by example they could better their lives after the divorce.

Courtney, age twenty-eight, said,

Whenever I feel like my life's out of control, I tell myself, "It's time to make lemonade out of a lemon!" Then I start to see things more clearly and focus on trying to solve my problems instead of groaning about them. I learned that from my mother—making lemonade out of lemons was her favorite saying. She grew up in Iowa in a family with five brothers and sisters. All of them had to pitch in to make their small farm work, so she learned that to survive, you had to personally take responsibility to do so. There were no excuses, since it was assumed by her hardworking parents that they all had to do their duties. It was good training for her, because life was hard after my dad left. She divorced him—he was a womanizer and left for another woman, but that relationship also broke up. I was thirteen at the time, just going into high school. The divorce hurt me because I loved both my mom and dad and was afraid I'd never be able to see my dad again after the divorce. But my parents had joint custody and made sure I would still see them both even though I lived with my mother. Luckily, my parents weren't vengeful people.

My dad paid child support, but it wasn't enough, so Mom had to worry about paying all the bills. She was determined to get a full forty-hour-a-week job after the divorce, which she did working as a saleslady in a big department store. She never complained; she just did it because, as she told me, it had to be done and no one else could be responsible for earning a salary but herself. It was sink or swim, and she preferred to swim. She later became, and still is, a sales buyer, a very successful one, at that same department store.

So, I learned early in life that was the way to go. Complaining gets you nowhere, it's the doing that counts. My mother only had a high school education and always wanted me to go to college. So when I graduated from my high school, it only seemed normal to me to go to college, which I did. Mom also taught me to be a compassionate person. She always has sympathy for people who have a harder time in life than she

*does. When she sees a homeless person on the street—and there
are so many of them in our city—she will always hand them
a dollar or two. She knows that what they need is community
care, but she says that when she hands them a little money it's
like making a statement that human beings need to care about
each other. So I think it was only natural for me, with that
kind of upbringing, to become a health educator in a hospital,
which I am. I graduated with a master's degree in the health
sciences and feel lucky to do what I am doing. I now have a
three-year-old daughter (my husband is a high school teacher)
and you can be sure I'm educating her in self-reliance—and
compassion—just like I was. I suppose my daughter will have
an easier time growing up than I did, because adjusting to my
parents' divorce was hard on me, but you never know. She will
also have lots of problems. That's what life presents all of us
with, problems that need to be confronted and solved. That's
what I'm teaching my daughter. The only alternative is to drift
through life and then wake up on your deathbed and ask, "Is
this all there is?" I want my daughter to live with her eyes wide
open. Life is too short to let it sift like sand through your
fingers.*

Building Self-Esteem

The ACDs we counsel are testaments to the truth of the observation the philosopher Nietzsche made more than one hundred years ago. He said, "What does not destroy me, makes me stronger."

Next to the death of an actual loved one, the most traumatic experience in a person's life is divorce. Divorce is also a death—the death of a relationship, the death of intimacy—which is experienced as an assault on one's own sense of self. The road beyond divorce can lead to disaster (even suicide or murder of one's ex-spouse, children, lawyers, or judges as newspaper headlines attest), or it can lead to an opportunity for self-renewal and a chance for greater happiness in life rather than endless despair.

The men and women in our ACD groups chose self-renewal and have embarked on a road to a brighter future for themselves. To do so required their dedication to rebuilding their own self-esteem. The initial effect of divorce is the lowering of one's self-esteem because a floodgate of mixed feelings (e.g., guilt, anger, hatred, vengeance, regret, sadness, self-pity, helplessness, or worthlessness) usually wash over a person in the earliest stages of divorce. The net effect of these feelings is the diminishing in the belief that the individual is a person of value and worth who is capable of making positive things happen now that the predivorce life has shattered. For these ACDs, taking personal responsibility for improving one's life is the first step toward building up self-esteem. This is the concept that the members of our groups believed was most essential to contribute to their own children's welfare.

It is possible for any ACD reading this book to successfully apply the same approach to his or her own life. The ACDs in our groups are average men and women, not superior creatures. That's what is so exciting about their achievements. What they required was a sense of hope, the willingness to seek out helping resources, and then the ability to act in ways to regain their sense of value and self-worth. They had to regain the notion that they are able to create healthy families for themselves. Their motivation was to act as people capable of making positive things happen in their lives, rather than passively waiting for the next disaster to occur.

As a role model of how self-esteem can arise from ground-zero feelings of worthlessness, we're reminded of Kathy, age forty-four. She is a woman who strives to make a paramount effort to enhance her children's self-esteem. She has two girls, ages sixteen and nineteen.

Why is self-esteem so important to me and my children? It's because without it I wouldn't even be alive today. There was a long time in my marriage I felt completely worthless. I felt I had no value as a human being, let alone value as a woman. I used to fight against killing myself. I knew I had made a mistake in the first year I married Joe, yet I stayed in that awful marriage for fourteen years because I believed divorce was a sin against God.

When I married Joe I didn't know he was an abused child who was molested by his uncle a dozen times when he was a kid. I found that out after my divorce. I thought I had made the right choice. He was the silent type, which I mistakenly interpreted as being thoughtful. You see, I grew up in a family of screamers. My parents never could agree and kept screaming at each other long after they divorced when I was sixteen. So I used to say to myself that when I grew up, I would never marry a man who always barks, like my dad used to do to my mother. After I married him, I discovered that Joe wasn't the strong silent thoughtful type I thought he was. He was silent because he had nothing interesting to say. And I always felt he was hiding something, like he had a dirty little secret he didn't want anyone to know about. Well that secret was the rapes by his uncle.

While I was married to Joe, he never talked to me, apart from complaints about how I didn't discipline our two girls or wasn't keeping the house clean enough. It was like I was his servant rather than a wife. He never—no not once—told me he loved me during the entire time we were married. Our sex life was a total disaster—I never experienced any tenderness, any desire on his part to pleasure me or participate in foreplay. He always went for home base. It was ten minutes of intercourse at the most and nothing else.

Joe was the manager of a small construction company and made good money. He didn't want me to work outside of the home, I suppose because he felt that would reflect badly on his manhood. But I really don't know, because he never said anything beyond the order for me to be only a homebody.

I was always trying to read his mind, because he was like a blank sheet of paper and I was desperate to fill in the blanks. As I said, I always put the blame on myself, that I was not a good wife, otherwise I would please him and he would say he loved me. But as hard as I tried to please him, his lack of response never changed. Whenever he did talk, it was always criticism of myself and the children. Never a word of praise.

Since I always placed the blame on myself—that I could never do anything right—I often thought of suicide. My self-esteem—as a person deserving to live—was then zero. The thing that prevented me from doing so was not only that I believed—and still do—that it was a sin against God, but that by killing myself, my children would be at the mercy of their father.

What saved my life—and my children's—was what I still believe was a gift from God. In my eleventh year of marriage I was totally desperate and confessed my problem to my church minister who was compassionate and knew about psychology. He didn't recommend either staying married or getting a divorce. He suggested instead that I see a good counselor and talk to him or her about my distress. He gave me the name of a psychotherapist, Dr. Gainer, who really saved my life. He counseled me for two years, twice a week.

I acknowledged to Dr. Gainer that I wanted to know what I could do to make the marriage better, but he told me only two persons willing to look at their behavior—unskillful behavior he called it—and change that behavior with the help of a counselor could make a marriage become happier. And he said that it could only happen if there was enough love left in a relationship. That was the most important thing he said to me. Because I realized there was no love left in my marriage to Joe, only my guilty feeling of being obligated to serve his needs at the expense of my own.

After three years of counseling, I had enough courage to file for divorce. I had nothing to fear about earning my own living since I did very well in computer work and there were plenty of available jobs in my field. What gave me the most courage to take this action was my concern for the health and happiness of my own daughters. My marriage had made both of them anxious and insecure—they saw me as a wimp and feared they would be the same when they grew up. Their self-esteem was also almost nothing and that frightened me.

Of course, my husband was angry when I filed for divorce. He didn't know that in my state one person could file for divorce even if the other didn't want it—it's called getting a divorce because of irreconcilable difficulties. He didn't want the divorce because it would mean he'd have to find another housekeeper and maid, which I was both. Well, that was what I had been, but when I divorced I wanted to become a wife who is loved for the person she is. Joe could never understand that.

That was seven years ago, and I got sole custody of my daughters. The divorce—and Dr. Gainer's counseling—saved all three of our lives. Two years ago I married a great guy, Chris. He's three years older than me and was a widower— his wife died seven years ago. Chris never had children and treats my girls as if they were his own (my ex never even attempted to see his two girls again). Chris also cherishes me as much as I cherish him. That's what self-esteem is all about. It's believing you count for something in this world instead of feeling like you're disposable tissue paper.

So it's no small wonder that I always try to nurture my own girls' self-esteem. I tell them that they are entitled to be treated with respect for who they are and when they get married they should marry an equal partner, not a person superior or inferior to them. And because of my own sexual nightmare with Joe, I've had long talks with them about what to look for in a good sexual relationship. First of all, I tell them that sex in marriage should be an expression of a good interpersonal relationship, rather than a substitute for such a relationship. It's a celebration about how good you feel about your relationship, rather than just a physical charge.

The girls see how Chris and I relate to each other. The way Chris acts sexually with me touches a part of my soul I didn't know existed when I lived with Joe. With Chris, sex is about caring for each other, being attentive to each other's needs and believing you really count as a person of value and worth and are respected for being exactly that. You can't feel like a person of value and worth if you are emotionally abused by your mate. For that's what Joe did to me, emotionally abused me by never respecting my needs and putting me down all the time. Dr. Gainer drew that to my attention and said emo-

tional abuse can feel even more harmful than physical abuse. Dr. Gainer made me aware of that for the first time in my life. He was certainly right in my case.

I now regard self-esteem as being a necessity of life. Without it, I would just be a person without spirit, without hope— I would be back in my marriage with Joe.

ACDs strive to incorporate the qualities enumerated in Kathy's story in their own parenting, and they can be used by anyone who wishes to work on his or her parenting skills. For those of you who are divorced and raising young children—and those ACDs who are contemplating having children—the hard-earned knowledge of the men and women who have generously shared their own experiences in the previous pages may indeed be helpful.

Eight Guidelines for Skillful Parenting as Practiced by Adult Children of Divorce

The following list offers eight guidelines to summarize the ways in which adult children of divorce try to nurture their children in constructive ways. These are not limited to the divorce experience and can be applied by any parent who wishes to use them. In fact, utilizing these eight guidelines can be an excellent divorce-prevention prescription as well as improving post-divorce living relationships.

1. **Each child is a unique individual.** He or she is not the clone of the mother or father or any other family member. Every

person on earth is unique and needs validation of his or her individuality. Never stereotype a child by saying and believing he or she is the "spitting image" of some member of your family and then attributing the same qualities and abilities (or lack of them) these family members have to your children!

2. **Children need to be permitted to express all of their feelings.** Never tell a child all of their feelings must be judged on a scale of being "good" or "bad." Feelings in themselves are neither good nor bad. They exist to be understood, not judged. For example, anger is not a "bad" feeling; it may be a cover for being fearful. The fear has to be resolved rather than condemned. Listen to all of what your children's feelings are telling you. They are clues to how you can be most helpful to them.

3. **Never call your child "bad" if his or her behavior is out of line.** It's one thing to let him or her know the behavior is unacceptable; it's quite another to say he or she is a "bad person," which lowers his or her self-esteem. Many ACDs grew up with the constant voices of their parents telling them they were "rotten kids," "bad apples," or "stupid." They will have none of this bad-mouthing in their own families. As one woman in our group said, "When my nine-year-old daughter says she won't do the dishes, I tell her, 'I love you and I know you don't want to do the dishes, but even if you hate doing them, that's the family chore you said you would do, so you must do them.' I don't tell her she's a rotten kid because she doesn't want to do the dishes."

4. **Don't ever put the "I'm bigger than you are, so you better do what I say" burden on your children.** Children need reasons for doing what you may require them to do. Even if they don't like doing something you may want them to do, they are

entitled to the reasons why you believe it must be done. Their intelligence needs to be respected.

5. **Nurture your children's ability to take personal responsibility for their behavior and be accountable to themselves for their performance.** This value is near and dear to each ACDs' heart, because each learned early in life that the only way he or she could better his or her life was to take personal responsibility to make positive things happen. This was one of the most valuable learning experiences each ACD wished to transmit to his or her children.

6. **Time is the most precious commodity you can give your children.** To rear children who can be proud of themselves as well as you being proud of them, you need to give them what your parents never gave you—personal, caring time. It demonstrates love that tells children that they are valuable enough for you to share yourself with them. You can buy mountains of material things for your children, but what they will remember most as they grow up is "the time my mom and dad spent with me, which showed me how important they thought I was." This is the loving recollection of their parents they will treasure for life. If you were deprived of this gift of time from your own parents, you now have a second chance to enjoy that experience through nurturing your children.

7. **Strive for success rather than prosperity.** We live in mean-spirited times which is all the more reason to teach your children how to lead a successful, rather than a prosperous life if they are to experience happiness in their grown-up years. Because adult children of divorce have experienced much adversity in their lives, many of them have developed great compassion

for the underprivileged, the poor, the sick, and the emotionally walking wounded. They choose professions that are helpful to society and give such people a "hand up" rather than a "handout." We have many social workers, psychologists, health-care providers, environmentalists, educators, and social scientists in our ACD groups. None of these men and women places making money as their highest priority in life. They strive to achieve a "successful" rather than a "prosperous" life.

To be prosperous is to be "rich" in material things—the big bank accounts, the investments, the trendy cars and vacations, or the biggest house on the block. On the other hand, being successful validates the need for economic security, but not at the expense of all of the other nonmaterial aspects of life that create happiness. When money and power become obsessive ends in themselves, your children can waste away from emotional malnutrition. The poet Wallace Stevens once said that life is an affair of people, not of things. To forget that is to forget that marriage and the nurturing of children is based on love, mutual respect, empathy, and caring. That is the real bottom line. It is encouraging to know that so many adult children of divorce are transmitting this knowledge to their children.

8. **Be resourceful.** The strong person seeks out help to solve difficult problems. Our culture has many avenues to assist you if you are concerned with problems of parenting, divorce, career choices, or psychological and addictive problems. These are examples of a wide range of resources you can use for self-renewal (e.g., counseling experts, social service organization, community college education, libraries, and the Internet). Many of these resources are free or cost little. Tap into your potential strength for improving your life.

8

The Struggle for Kindness

When the great writer-philosopher Aldous Huxley was dying, he was asked what words of wisdom and advice he would like to leave to the world. He replied, "I wish people would be kinder to each other."

When we read Huxley's advice to the members of our ACD groups we always get the same response. Both men and women react with poignant sadness, and their eyes often glisten with held-back tears. They recall that kindness was nonexistent in the growing-up period of their lives. And oh! How they yearned for their parents to show more kindness to them and each other.

We would then read to them the extended *American Heritage Dictionary* definition of what it means to be "kind." Here is what it says: "Of a friendly nature; generous or hospitable; warm-hearted; good; charitable; helpful; showing sympathy or understanding; humane; considerate; tolerant."

The very fact that all of these qualities were only dreams that were rarely, if ever, experienced in their early years, made the ACDs in our groups all the more determined to make them realities in their own grown-up lives. They are acutely aware that these are the qualities they should present and imprint in their own children and practice in their interpersonal relationships.

We tell them it's all right to feel sad and even weep for the kindness they didn't receive as a child. But then they should let go of regret and use their present lives as a second chance to experience these qualities.

Choosing Kindness

Aldous Huxley saw the world as a very unkind place when he made his recommendation. That was in 1964. If he had lived until today, he might believe little has changed because endless wars seem to be the defining reality of this new century. At this beginning of the new millennium, the practice of kindness in our life resembles a drought. Meanness, rudeness, four-letter word arguments, violent confrontations, road rage, and mistrust pervade our daily life outside the home. National TV programs devote segments of their shows to exploiting the prevalence of nastiness in our society. Turn to any number of TV talk shows and screaming confrontations are their daily bread. As for talk radio shows, name-calling, sneers, discourtesy, and slander define much of their content. To hear a "thank you" from a clerk—or an apology for a mistake made—is as frequent as snow falling on Los Angeles. Courtesy on the highway is a thing of the past. It is difficult to remain uncontaminated by this gross insensitivity, so we often bring some of it home when we leave the office.

It is within the context of this temper of our times that adult children of divorce have to struggle twice as hard to practice or receive kindness. Yet, if we really look, the kindness is there—in others and in ourselves. Here is what Denise, a thirty-six-year-old mother of three, whose parents divorced when she was ten, says:

I so wanted a hug, a kiss, a thank-you from my parents, but neither of them ever did that to each other, so what right did I expect that they would do that to me? I used to be in the top 5 percent of my class, but they never once said, "Well done, here's a kiss and a hug and let's go out and celebrate," when I came home with a straight-A report card. So when I left home and married and had my three girls, I was determined to never repeat what happened to me. I thought that was going to be easy—but you know what?—it turned out to be very difficult. Just because I thought I would do exactly the opposite of what my parents did to me didn't mean it could happen automatically. My husband, Jeff, is exactly the opposite—he came from a huggy-kissy family, received lots of praise as a kid, and was always told to be courteous and remember thank yous. I love that in him, he's so good at that with the kids and me. But I've had trouble from the beginning of our marriage to accept a spontaneous hug, a love pat, or a surprise kiss from my husband, just for their own sake. At first, it was so foreign to my experience. Because such signs of spontaneous affection were never what I received when I was a kid, it felt almost like a physical attack, rather than a sign of love from Jeff, which indeed it was. I was experiencing what that old warning said, "Don't ask for what you want, you're liable to get it!"

That reaction has pretty well disappeared by now, and I've learned to emotionally, not only intellectually, like those loving gestures of Jeff. But still, I have to be aware of a certain resistance to my hugging and kissing my kids the way I wanted to be hugged. It's like I'm acting like my mother used to act. It's as if she's still in my mind, even though she's long dead.

I've learned to tell myself again and again that I am not my mother and that I have a right to give and receive hugs

*and kisses and praise. You see when I was growing up I felt—
wrongly—that I wasn't entitled to any signs of affection; if my
parents never gave me any it was because I didn't deserve any.*

What Denise said confirms what T. S. Eliot once reflected,
that between the thought and the act falls the shadow. The
"shadow" that inhibited Denise is the difference between what
she intellectually wanted to do and what her past upbringing prevented her from emotionally doing. However, once she got in
touch with why she was experiencing such resistance to the very
thing she wanted to do, she was able to overcome it. But residue
from everyone's upbringing remains for years and years after one
leaves his or her parents' home. Consequently, Denise will have
to continue to monitor her behavior if she is to fully enjoy what
her parents never permitted her to experience.

Resolving the Past with Kindness

The thrust for coming to terms with one's family of origin is very
prevalent in adult children of divorce. When it comes to con-
fronting their past relationship with their own divorced parents,
ACDs hope to lay the past to rest and to drain themselves of the
remembered hurt, pain, anger, rejection, isolation, and loneliness
that still invade their sleep, even after the death of both parents.
To prevent the remembered pain of the past from controlling
their present life, many adult children of divorce have not hesi-
tated to seek out a good therapist, psychologist, or psychoanalyst.

As a result of therapy, most of the ACDs in our group did
indeed come to a constructive resolution of their conflicted feelings about their parents' personalities, their divorce, and the lack
of kindness the ACD experienced. One of our clients, Paul, a

forty-three-year-old advertising executive, expressed his problem in a way that was typical of many ACDs. "My parents were the people who created me, and so as I was growing up they were the people I loved the most. But they were also the ones I hated the most because I felt they were harming me and yet I felt guilty as hell for hating them, even though I thought they deserved my hatred."

How to resolve this dilemma? Remaining angry was no solution. The German dramatist Bertolt Brecht said he kept a Japanese carving of the mask of an evil demon in his room. He said he looks at the swollen veins of the demon's forehead to remind him what a terrible strain it is to be evil. It is an equal strain to harbor ongoing anger and hatred. As one ACD remarked, "If I continue to act angry, cruel, and vengeful, I become just like my father—the very thing I've always wanted to avoid!"

With few exceptions, the ACDs who went into therapy were able to view their parents in an entirely different light. They now saw their mother and father with their *adult* eyes, not their child's eyes. When they were still evaluating their parents as if they themselves were still the hurt child passing judgment on parents who caused them pain, they could not rid themselves of remembered anguish. However, viewing their parents from the vantage point of their adult intelligence, insight, and experience, they were able to become compassionate instead of vengeful—and they recalled their past family life with understanding.

Seeing Your Parents in a New Light

Believing is perception. The more you understand about your parents' behavior, the more you will see them in a new light. What you may have believed as a child (e.g., you were unlovable or your parents were deliberately selfish and uncaring) may totally change when you learn why they acted the way they did in their marriage, rather than attribute malicious intent to their behavior toward themselves or you. Your judgment can change when your knowledge increases.

Your Parents Were Probably Unskilled Rather Than Intending to Do Harm to Themselves and Their Children

They knew no better and had no knowledge of resources that could help them solve their problems more skillfully.

Violence Often Stemmed from Ignorance

If parents of ACDs were violent, that was often the way their own parents and families tried to solve their problems. So the ACD learns to see that physical violence was their unskillful attempt to resolve arguments, rather than continuing to believe that the parent "enjoyed" harming the family. The parent had learned this behavior from his or her own parents and so believed this was the "normal" way to get family members to agree with each other.

Alcoholism Was Not Known to Be an Addiction

If alcoholism was rampant in their family of origin, today ACDs are armed with the knowledge that it is an addiction—not a sign of personal evil as they once thought while they were growing up. Many ACDs learned their parents (sometimes both their mother and father) had a genetic inheritance that predisposed them to alcohol addiction. Their parents never knew this, and many deluded themselves that they could "handle" their liquor and thought they had no need to get help such as Alcoholics Anonymous because they either had no access to these programs or viewed them as places where only "losers" go.

Physical and Mental Illnessses Were Often Unidentified and Untreated

Some of the ACDs had parents who suffered from undetected illnesses for many years. And it was the illness itself that created the havoc in their family life that ended in divorce, not vicious intent. One of our clients, Ted, a thirty-eight-year-old Web master, shared with us a poignant insight he recently experienced that changed his attitude of hatred toward his long-dead father to compassion. Ted recently discovered a diary his mother left at the time of her death. He showed us her notations in the diary that caused him to dramatically change his perspective about his father, and he allowed us to share his mother's notes with you:

> *One of the most painful realizations about my marriage that I have come to is the utter isolation I feel from my husband. I felt it almost immediately after we were married. It seemed like there was an invisible wall that I couldn't penetrate. If I got too close to the wall or tried to break through it, my husband became angry and aggressive and basically shooed me away. At first I was terribly hurt by this and felt unloved. Then it turned to anger and I tried to live my life concurrently with him but with little interaction of significance. In other words, his indifference became my own.*

His drug and alcohol abuse is another way, I feel, he isolates himself. He enjoys those very private spaces that can only belong to himself. He excludes others from deeply sharing an experience, and often the memory lapses further alienate any desire to try to get close. It feels demeaning that I share myself only to find out later that my husband was drunk or high. Sexually, it makes me feel like a whore since I share my body with someone who isn't really there. And each form of high shows a different part of his personality, which makes it very confusing to know which husband is home at night—the alcoholic, the drug user, or the worn-out workaholic.

The end result of being forced to live on the edge of my husband's life has resulted in my feeling I was living a life that was hopeless and without any joy. I, too, use alcohol now because I feel so alone, but it has only made my marriage even worse, because we now have two self-contained bubbles colliding. Communication of any real depth has long since gone and centers now more on business and coping than significant feelings, plans for our children and for the future. My memory also has been affected by drinking. My blackouts are a safe place of refuge. Unfortunately, memory lapses have become ammunition in a subtle verbally abusive war that is being waged between us.

Now that I am trying to eliminate drinking from my life, I see that it is very often not my memory but his which is faulty, this being corroborated by several friends and family. I see how worn out I am living in the roller coaster ride of his life. The perpetual seeking of highs—with drugs, work, aggressive drinking, loud music, incessant watching of television action movies—describing his world in terms of black-and-white, right-and-wrong, there are no grays, no "down" time,

*no maybes. As his spouse, it's exhausting. Emotionally, I live
in a wasteland. I don't have any expectation of him to query
about my life as his totally absorbs him. I don't feel precious
anymore, but feel that each day is an ordeal and I don't even
anticipate his coming home anymore because of his erratic
schedule which changes on a whim.*

"It's so sad," Ted said to us after we had read these notes.
"Mom and Dad both didn't know that Dad was suffering from
a disease that prevented him from demonstrating his love for
the family. Mom thought she was unlovable because of his
behavior, and Dad thought he was doing the best he could,
because he was a good wage earner. He was a talented brokerage
salesman. I now know—which my parents never did—that he
had a disease."

Ted's father had the classic signs of the disease now known as
adult attention deficit disorder. It is a problem that can be identified by doctors and psychologists and managed by medication
and psychological counseling. We have helped many couples in
stressful marriages lead happy lives once we informed them that
the husband (or wife) had an attention deficit disorder disease
and helped that spouse connect with knowledgeable doctors
who could put them in a managed medication program. The
combination of managed medication and psychological counseling by us could—and does—turn stressful marriages into happy
ones if this disease had been the unknown cause of their marital problems. But when Ted's mother wrote her diary notes, she
and her husband were living in a time when adult attention
deficit disorder was an unknown disease. Six months after Ted's
mother wrote the last sentences in her diary, she left his father
and divorced him. Ted and his sister, Jan, lived with their mother.

"That was twenty-five years ago when I was thirteen," Ted recalled, "and I never saw my father again. He wasted away and died of heart failure five years after Mom left him."

Ted kept repeating, "It's so sad, so sad," and then tears flooded his eyes. He later told us that he had cried his hatred and bitterness against his father out of his system on that day he told us this story. "How can I hate my father! He was such a tragic figure, not the bastard I thought he was," Ted said.

Ted had transformed himself into a compassionate son.

We don't all find such illuminating diaries, but it's now well known that attention deficit disorder, depression, and other diseases struck families so harshly because people were not aware of them, or of treatments for them. This could have been the case for your own parents. So try to judge them with compassion and get help if you see them begin to display any dysfunctional symptoms.

Economic Circumstances and Lack of Opportunity Often Crushed Good People

Some ACDs discovered that their parents were trapped by circumstances that caused them to act hurtfully toward their family. Some parents felt self-hatred because they could not find a well-paying job that could support their family. They projected their self-hatred on to their spouse and children, who had to suffer their abuse. Many ACDs lived in families where their mothers led unfulfilled lives. They felt they were trapped housewives when they wanted careers of their own. And there were the parents, usually fathers, who literally hated their jobs, but felt they had no other alternative but to remain in them because they were the only breadwinners and couldn't let their family starve. Their only outlet was to vent their frustration on their family because they couldn't do that to their boss.

These were well-intentioned parents who were victims of forces beyond their control. Society did not provide them with the resources they needed to escape their economic frustrations. They had the misfortune of living in times when the economy was being downsized and hundreds of thousands of workers were being laid off, and in times when gender stereotypes defined one's role in life and in a marriage.

Once these facts were understood, the ACDs who experienced living in households with such parents, began to regard their parents as struggling human beings who may have been unskillful in dealing with life's problems, but were by no means the cruel persecutors they once envisioned them to be.

Sometimes, Understanding Just Isn't Possible but Healing Is

Of course, some of the ACDs emerged from therapy with no change in attitude toward their parents. There are indeed people in this world who enjoy being vicious, cruel, and punitive, who delight in hurting people. Sadists of this type are rare, but they do exist. And for these ACDs, who only had their child-based judgment that a parent was indeed a sadist affirmed in therapy, then all that could be done was to weep for the parent they never had and then move their lives forward without reliving their past. Their therapy was of great help to them in working toward this resolution. They at least came to understand that it was not their doing that the parent was that way.

Many Parents Were Overly Strict from a Misguided Sense of Love

Some ACDs learned in therapy that the parents who they thought were uncaring had indeed been very concerned about their welfare. These ACDs had misinterpreted the discipline from the parent with whom they lived after the divorce as punishment. Now with adult eyes, they could value such a parent rather than disparage her or him. For example, Lisa, a forty-one-year-old clothes designer, told us of her reversed judgment of the parent she lived with after the divorce:

> My father left home and never came back when I was eleven and my younger brother, Tim, was six. Dad was a womanizer; he paid more attention to the women he would pick up than my mother or myself or Tim. When he left us, we never heard from him again. I used to hear my mother sobbing in her room and I would feel very scared. I would think, if my father left us, what would my mother do? Maybe my brother and I would become orphans!
>
> That didn't happen, of course. My mother stopped sobbing after awhile and she became very stern with me. She told me I was to take care of our apartment when she wasn't home and that I was responsible for seeing that nothing happened to Tim. She had to work eight hours a day as a secretary to support us, since we never received a cent from my father. Just paying the rent was a struggle for her.
>
> I felt I was a burden to her—just another mouth to feed. She would criticize me for the slightest mistake I made. If I spilled a drop of milk on the floor, she went ballistic; if I didn't do my homework on time, she called me lazy; she would call me "stupid" if I had one C on my report card even though I

had three As in addition. I never was praised, even when I made the apartment spic-and-span and always washed the dishes on time. She said that was expected of me, so why should she congratulate me for a job well done?

There was an incident that stayed with me all my life. It was the time when I was twelve and fell in the school yard during lunch hour and cut my right knee. I ran home frightened because blood was coming out. My mother was home that afternoon and I was crying and afraid. Maybe my leg would be amputated. My mother didn't pay attention to my crying, but immediately wiped away the blood with some soap and water and put a Band-Aid on the cut. "There's nothing to cry about," she told me, "so stop crying. It's just a little cut and wasn't deep at all. It should heal by tomorrow. But you can go back to school now, since it won't hurt you. You're OK."

I went back to school, but for some reason I felt very hurt. I should have been happy because it was just a minor cut and my mother fixed it, but I wasn't. I never could understand why I couldn't forget that incident, since it was so minor and I had other accidents as a kid, like all kids have them, and yet I forgot them quickly. I found out later in therapy why this incident seemed so important to me.

I went to see a psychologist because my eldest son, Ben (who is twenty-one and is a history major in a college a thousand miles from where I live), never came home to visit me during the holidays or during his summer vacations. He would always say he had a term paper to finish—that it was overdue and he needed the time for additional research. It was always the same story, always the same excuses and I got tired of them. So I wrote him a long letter that asked, was he being truthful or trying to avoid seeing me? His answer shocked me. He told me he was always making excuses because it was too painful

*for him to come home. When he saw me, he complained that
I never asked about how he was feeling, or was he happy or
depressed or worried about his relationships. It was only about
what his grades were and what plans he was making to get a
career and how he was spending his allowance. He said he felt
I didn't care about him as a person because I was always talking to him or at him, telling him what to do, but never asking how he was feeling or what he wanted rather than what
I wanted. He said he loved me and didn't want to hurt me,
but felt I deserved an honest answer since I asked for one.*

*When I read his letter, I said to myself, "My God, he's made
me out to be just like my mother." My mother did the same
thing to me and I felt as a kid just like Ben. In the back of my
mind, I knew my mother loved me—after all she took care of
me after my father left—but the way she treated me seemed
so unfair.*

*When I told my psychologist all of this, he helped me
understand my mother better and changed my relationship
with Ben, because I began to act differently from the cold fish
he thought I was.*

*I've changed now. The memory of that cut on my knee has
disappeared. I keep making every effort to fight this tendency
to only concern myself with my kids' performance, rather than
how they are doing as whole persons. It's the quality of their
entire life, not just a part of it, that's important for me to be
concerned about. And that's the way I relate to my kids now.
Oh, yes, Ben likes to visit with me now! Luckily, it wasn't too
late.*

*I wish I could tell my mother today how much I love her
and respect her for all the sacrifices she made. But that can't
happen. You see, she has Alzheimer's, so when I visit with her
in the hospital the most I can do is to hug and kiss her and*

hold her hand, since she only recognizes me part of the time and is fading fast. I do tell her I love her, and even though she doesn't respond intelligently to what I'm saying, I feel sure that her spirit is hearing what I say.

When we heard these ACD life stories, we recalled the wonderful observation by the great English poet William Blake, "The eye altering alters all."

Translated into today's terminology, it tells us we can grow and change for the better—and become kinder—any time in our life, provided we have the willpower to do so. We change our world when we change the way we see things.

9

Creating a More
Compassionate Society

The adult children of divorce who have walked through the hot coals of family disruption and dysfunction, economic insecurity, and emotional disarray can and do prevail over the jolts life gave them. To prevail means to triumph over life's difficulties, to use them as learning experiences rather than as punishments because you are an ACD. Many ACDs have matured earlier in our society than others who grew up in allegedly more "fortunate" nondivorced households. They have learned early in life what all too many people never learn. That the only way to make positive things happen was by taking personal responsibility to make them happen. As Tom, an ACD research group member, said, "I remember one of the first things my mother told me when I was twelve, right after she divorced my father, who was an alcoholic, she said that the only things she and I could count on to make our lives better were our own right arm and our teamwork. And she was right."

Tom spoke with the authority of a person relying on his own efforts to become, at thirty-five, a successful computer consultant with a wife and two children. He's had some bumpy roads in his ten-year marriage but says it's better than ever now: "That's because when the going got rough, we went to a marriage counselor instead of getting a divorce. I suggested going, because that's what my mother did when she remarried my stepfather five years after she left my father. They're still together in a happy way. That's my mother, a real problem solver. No whining, no excuses."

What we have repeatedly seen validated in our research with adult children of divorce is a prevailing tendency of the majority to incorporate this sense of personal responsibility into the very fiber of who they are. In growing up, it was sink or swim against a tide of severe difficulties that they initially thought were the consequence of their parents' divorce—and it was those difficulties that they overcame. It was no accident that their adversity became a gift, because it taught them to take personal responsibility to act skillfully to overcome their problems. When I asked the group whether or not they still believed that the difficulties they experienced after their parents' divorce were primarily the product of that divorce, their answer was a surprise. They uniformly said, "no!" The reasons were many: unemployment, low-paying jobs, racial discrimination, no children, no health insurance, no decent affordable housing, second-hand clothes and beat-up toys, and feeling like an outsider.

Steve, a forty-year-old African-American lawyer, summed up the consensus of the group eloquently:

It wasn't the divorce when I was eight, that was just the consequence of my father abusing my mother. She saved her life by getting out of that marriage. Instead, society gave us no support. Because she was black, my mother could only get minimum wage jobs. She would have liked to get a career, but there were no resources available for her. When my two sisters and I were sick, there were no doctors since we had no money and no health insurance. We had to cure ourselves instead. Yes, I was discriminated against in school and called names. But that didn't make me feel bad because I always had the highest grades in my classes and knew I was better than those jerks who skipped school, smoked dope, and made fun of my skin color. It was my mother who said to me that getting a scholarship to college would be my way to success. She was right. I became a community lawyer. I specialize in helping people who were just like me and aren't lucky enough to escape the rotten conditions they live in. Let's face it, I never believed in the garbage the politicians tell us that it's all the fault of a divorce or of personal incompetence that prevents a person from living well. We all need a helping hand at some time in our lives—why, if there were no scholarships, I could never have gone to college. And I was lucky I didn't die when I had pneumonia as a kid, since we had no health insurance. Everyone should have health insurance, which is really a right to life that our society ought to supply us with. To talk about divorce being the big problem is absurd. It wasn't divorce that almost killed me as a kid—it was the lack of a doctor because we couldn't afford one.

Steve was talking with the passion of recalling the indignities he experienced in his early years. The others in the group didn't have to say anything. They just nodded their heads in approval of what he said.

"Round Up the Usual Suspects!"

When a foul deed is committed, the police captain in the film *Casablanca* says, "Round up the usual suspects!" Of course, "the usual suspects" are never the ones who committed the deed.

In our society, divorce has become "the usual suspect" in ascribing all of the negative consequences that can happen to children of divorce throughout their entire lifetime. However, the *real* culprit is right before our very eyes but is ignored. The overlooked suspect is our society itself, because it creates the conditions that define much of who we are and what we can do or achieve in life. It is up to us to take personal responsibility to grasp the opportunities that are available to us to achieve a well-lived life. But if the opportunities are limited or not available, then it makes no sense to blame the person who is victimized by the lack of opportunity for his or her inability to succeed in life. A child of divorce—adult or otherwise—is *not* diminished by divorce but by the society that inhibits any possibility for personal development. Neither divorce nor marriage are the culprits—although both at one time or another have been labeled by various groups in our culture as the major causes of society's problems.

It is helpful to remember that marriage was the "usual suspect" in the late 1960s and '70s. The media was replete with books and manifestos and alleged "authorities" proclaiming the permanent death of marriage because it was an evil patriarchal institution that was the cause of our misery. Like Mark Twain said when reading his obituary in a newspaper, that the announcement of his death was highly exaggerated—so, too, the death of marriage has proved to be exaggerated. Twice as many marriages compared to divorces still occur annually. Many of these marriages include commitments by adult children of divorce, who don't fear marriage (as conventional wisdom has it), but welcome it on a more thoughtful, mature basis than many of the men and women who marry after experiencing a non-divorced family upbringing.

In today's times, marriage once again has been reinstated and labeled "good." But divorce still maintains its stigma. Less so than in previous decades, but still in evidence, particularly when it comes to labeling adult children of divorce as "permanent losers."

As we have noted previously, both marriage and divorce in themselves are simply structures that are neutral—neither is good nor bad. Each can serve a purpose well when each is well-stocked rather than barren of substance. They are like empty bottles: pour good wine in them and they function excellently. Pour sour, worm-ridden wine in them and they will function badly. Whether the wine is good or bad will depend on how the vineyard cultivates the grapes for the wine. If neglected, the vineyard will produce a bad crop; if nourished appropriately, a fine crop results.

Similarly, how can children of divorce flourish if in divorced households there is always the worry of losing a job; wages that can't support a family; fear of sickness because there is no health insurance; fear of becoming older because of age discrimination in the workplace; an unfair wage gender gap where women receive only 75 percent of what men receive for the same work; a polluted environment that makes one hesitate about bringing children into this world; and racial discrimination that continues to exist.

A "Hand Up," Not a "Handout"

Our society needs to reinforce the values of equality, compassion, empathy, generosity, and trust rather than mean-spirited discrimination against adult children of divorce. This substantial group in our society can make a major contribution to its improvement. Adult children of divorce know that people in adversity—like they were in their earlier years—need a hand up, not a handout. They know that government, just like marriage or divorce, is neither good nor bad—the uses government are put to define its positive or negative contribution to the welfare of its people. The kind of government they desire is a compassionate government.

Because of the adversity many adult children of divorce have experienced in their early years, they are in general wiser to the ways the interest groups that monopolize the media try to blind people about the value of government. The very corporate spokespeople who claim government is "bad" are the hirelings of the corporations that benefit the most by extracting from the government hundreds of millions of dollars in subsidies, tax exemptions, and legislation that accelerates the concentration of wealth to a small elite group (the census bureau affirms that 20 percent of the population owns 80 percent of the wealth of our country!).

Now that we are in the early years of the new millennium, it is appropriate to reapply the values of the Declaration of Independence and our Constitution, which affirmed more than two centuries ago that liberty, equality, and justice for *all* the people (not just a favored few) is the foundation of our democracy. We are the government—all the people, not just the wealthy lobbyists that buy our congresspersons.

Cynicism pervades our society today. The low turnout in elections affirms this, as do the ongoing spate of corporate scandals.

However, the most positive persons in our society indeed are the men and women who have triumphed over great adversity, such as the adult children of divorce. They know through hard-earned experience, positive things can happen if you make the effort to make them happen. On the other hand, cynicism is simply another form of hopelessness, which means allowing one's victimizers to continue to control one's life and to eliminate the possibilities of bettering one's place in society.

In our work and research with adult children of divorce, most seem to possess healthy skepticism when viewing politics or our culture. As twenty-eight-year-old, department store executive Kimberly told the group, "When I was a kid of fifteen, I knew that the media were telling me a lot of B.S. The six o'clock news was saying our economy was wonderful and there was no unemployment, yet my mother couldn't get a job for God knows how long because she was too old—she was forty-three and a damn good secretary. After that, I took what the media were telling me with a grain of salt." Kimberly's disenchantment with the media didn't discourage her from improving her condition in life; it just made her wiser and more mature earlier than most people, enabling her to make more skillful decisions to better her life. She questioned opinions rather than believing them to be true just because they were spoken by an alleged "authority."

Consequently, healthy skepticism affirms the possibility of using the democratic mechanisms in our society to create a better world for ourselves and our families in spite of those corporation and political forces that have their own agenda rooted in greed and power and who believe they can manipulate the rest of society for their own benefit.

A Compassionate Agenda for the Twenty-First Century

It is ironic and sad that we who live in the wealthiest society history has ever known still have so much unfinished business at hand when it comes to ensuring the well-being of all of our population. Yet a compassionate agenda does exist that is practical, sensible, and capable of becoming a reality when the majority of our population will make a concerted effort to make it happen.

When we showed this agenda to the ACD group members at our Creative Divorce, Love & Marriage Counseling Center Conferences, without first identifying who created it, they thought it was a very modern agenda that was appropriate to sponsor in our new century. They were very much surprised to learn that this agenda was announced sixty years ago. None other than President Franklin Delano Roosevelt, the most admired twentieth-century president, proclaimed this agenda as the unfinished business that American society needed to put into practice. Here is what he said in a speech dated January 12, 1944:

> *Human kindness has never weakened the stamina or softened the fiber of a free people. A nation does not have to be cruel in order to be tough. The vigorous expression of our American community spirit is truly important.*
>
> *The ancient injunction to love thy neighbor as thyself is still the force that animates our faith—a faith that we are determined shall live and conquer in a world poisoned by hatred and ravaged by war. . . .*
>
> *Government has a final responsibility for the well-being of its citizenship. If private cooperative endeavor fails to provide work for willing hands and relief for the unfortunate, those suffering hardship from no fault of their own have a right to call upon the government for aid; and a government worthy of its name must make fitting response. . . .*
>
> *We have come to a clear realization of the fact that true individual freedom cannot exist without economic security*

and independence. Necessitous men are not free men. People who are hungry and out of a job are the stuff of which dictatorships are made;

In our day these economic truths have become accepted as self-evident. We have accepted, so to speak, a second Bill of Rights under which a new basis of security and prosperity can be established for all, regardless of station, race or creed;

Among these are:

The right to a useful and remunerative job in the industries or shops or farms or mines of the nation;

The right to earn enough to provide adequate food and clothing and recreation;

The right of every farmer to raise and sell his products at a return which will give him and his family a decent living;

The right of every businessman, large and small, to trade in an atmosphere of freedom from unfair competition and domination by monopolies at home or abroad;

The right of every family to a decent home;

The right to adequate medical care and the opportunity to achieve and enjoy good health;

The right to adequate protection from the economic fears of old age, sickness, accident and unemployment;

All of these rights spell security . . . we must be prepared to move forward, in the implementation of these rights, to new goals of human happiness and well being.

President Roosevelt did not apologize for the need to create and maintain a compassionate society. Instead, he proudly accepted that fact. The beginning of the twenty-first century is an appropriate time to make Franklin Delano Roosevelt's twentieth-century compassionate agenda the finished business of our century.

Adult children of divorce who have refused to see themselves as victims accept this unfinished business compassionate agenda as a road map for creating a good life for themselves and their families. "Doesn't everyone feel the same way?" the ACDs in our research groups have asked us.

No, everyone doesn't. But they should!

Epilogue

The Positive Legacy of Adult Children of Divorce

The experiences you have lived through as an adult child of divorce have made you stronger rather than weaker. You have proved by your actions the truthfulness of the saying, "What does not destroy me makes me stronger." There is wisdom in overcoming adversity, which adult children of divorce are adept at doing.

You can be proud of what you have learned about life in spite of your background. You can validate your self-image by noting your accomplishments. Here is a list of them:

1. You have learned to survive in the face of profound difficulties.
2. You have not only "survived" but prevailed over these difficulties by achieving a more fulfilling existence than your parents.
3. You have recognized that it is your own personal responsibility to make positive things happen in your life.
4. You have developed a greater understanding and tolerance of diverse people precisely because you were exposed to a variety of people by virtue of your parents' divorce.
5. You have developed an awareness that problems in your personal life can be resolved if you go to counseling to

prevent them from victimizing you. The strong person goes to counseling.

6. You have learned that life is a series of crises and opportunities. You trust your self-reliance and resilience to triumph over them and take advantage of the opportunities.

7. It was John F. Kennedy who once remarked, "Life is unfair," and his own murder exemplified this concept. As an adult child of divorce, you have lived the reality of what he said and learned through hard experience that no one but yourself can mitigate that unfairness. This reality enables you to make the rest of your life healthier, happier, and fairer.

Resources for Self-Renewal

Recommended Reading

Thousands of books on divorce and personal relationships are in current publication. However, we are listing only those books that have proved most helpful to the adult children of divorce in our counseling practice and might be of equal benefit to you:

Bolles, Richard A. *What Color Is Your Parachute?* Berkeley, CA: Ten Speed Press, 2000.

Boston's Women's Health Collective. *Our Bodies, Ourselves.* New York: Touchstone Books, 1998.

Bruer, John T. *The Myth of the First Three Years: A New Understanding of Early Brain Development and Lifelong Learning.* New York: Free Press, 1999.

Cerf, Christopher, and Victor Navasky. *The Experts Speak.* New York: Pantheon Books, 1984.

Copnick, Alison, Andrew H. Meltzoff, and Patricia Kuhl. *The Scientist in the Crib: Minds, Brains, and How Children Learn.* New York: William Morrow, 1999.

Davis, Samson, George Jenkins, and Rameck Hunt. *The Pact: Three Young Men Make a Promise and Fulfill a Dream.* New York: Riverhead Books, 2002.

Fromm, Erich. *To Have or to Be?* New York: Continuum, 1996.

Gardner, Howard. *Frames of Mind: The Theory of Multiple Intelligence.* New York: Basic Books, 1983.

Harris, Judith Rich. *The Nurture Assumption.* New York: Free Press, 1998.

Hetherington, E. Mavis, and John Kelly. *For Better or for Worse: Divorce Reconsidered.* New York: W. W. Norton & Co., 2002.

Jampolsky, Gerald G. *Love Is Letting Go of Fear.* Berkeley, CA: Celestial Arts, 1979.

Krantzler, Mel. *Learning to Love Again.* New York: Harper Collins, 1987.

Krantzler, Mel and Melvin Belli. *Divorcing.* New York: St. Martins Press, 1992.

Krantzler, Mel and Patricia. *The New Creative Divorce.* Holbrook, MA: Adams Media Corp, 1998.

Le Shan, Lawrence. *How to Meditate.* New York: Bantam, 1974.

May, Rollo. *Love and Will.* New York: Dell Publishing Co., 1989.

Peck, M. Scott, M.D. *The Road Less Traveled.* New York: Simon and Schuster, 1978.

Rambo, Lewis R. *The Divorcing Christian.* Nashville: Abingdon Press, 1983.

Rowe, John W., M.D., and Robert L. Kahn, M.D. *Successful Aging.* New York: Pantheon Books, 1998.

Young, James J., C.S.P. *Divorcing, Believing, Belonging.* Ramsey, NJ: Paulist Press, 1984.

Zilbergeld, Bernard. *The New Male Sexuality.* New York: Bantam, 1999.

Recommended Websites for the Personal Growth of Adult Children of Divorce

"Search and you shall find." That could be the motto of the Internet, because millions of items of information and observations are available with the click of a mouse.

For ACDs, the Internet is a vital source of ongoing information on issues that are central to the personal growth and welfare for themselves, their children, and their extended families. However, the Internet will not automatically make persons the best informed that they can possibly be. In and of itself it can be a source of confusion and misinformation if not selectively used.

Consequently, there is the need for a sorting out of recommendations for your Internet use so that the gold of worthwhile information can be accessed without confusion from the dross of false or misleading information that tends to overwhelm worldwide websites. With this objective in mind, and operating from the principle that truthfulness and usefulness of what you find on the Internet is of paramount importance, we are listing websites that we believe can be of most help to ACDs. This list is arranged by topics that we believe are of greatest importance to ACDs. These websites are recommended as sites that can stimulate independent thinking. They are not designed to influence you to a biased way of thinking. Instead, they are designed to expand your horizons to think about the issues they present: you will decide what is useful in these sites to apply in your own life, not anyone else.

The sites we recommend are not overwhelming in number. They are useful guides that can also link you with many other sites that might interest you. You can use many of them to connect with other Internet site users who may have interests similar to yours through chat rooms, forums, instant messaging, and E-mails.

Exploring the Internet in this fashion can be an exciting journey: the world is at your disposal!

The most helpful search engine is Google (google.com). Google is the search engine of choice for ACDs to use for quality information on all phases of divorce life, as well as countless other issues of vital importance to your personal development.

Once you access Google, just type in the keywords "children of divorce," then click "Google search," and the search engine will immediately report back to you that there are nearly a million websites available for your perusal on this subject! Out of this gigantic well of information, the following websites might prove most helpful to you. We will also list websites other than those relating solely to divorce issues, because no ACD is simply a "product of divorced parents." He or she is a whole person, so the focus of our subsequent website recommendations will also include issues that enhance the growth of an entire person. It is the whole person that must cope with divorce issues, not a stereotype, if one is to move one's life into new stages of fulfillment.

• **American Association for Marriage and Family Therapy (aamft.org).** This prestigious organization is an excellent starting point for exploring divorce. This site also enables you to locate a reputable professional family counselor near you should you need one. (More than 15,000 licensed marriage and family therapists are listed.) This site also provides excellent sources of information on books, articles, and family problems.

• **Big Brothers/Big Sisters of America (bbsa.org).** Big Brothers/Big Sisters provides adult friends who serve as responsible mentors and role models for children in need. It is an excellent resource for divorced parents who need the help of positive adult role models for their children.

- **Dads and Daughters (dadsanddaughters.org)**. The slogan of this website is "Inspire, Understand, and Support your Daughter." This is a unique website that celebrates the father-daughter connection. It is a national education and advocacy nonprofit organization designed to strengthen father-daughter relationships and enhance the self-esteem of daughters.

- **The Department of Health and Human Services (hhs .gov)**. This outstanding website, designed by our government, demonstrates that our taxpayers' money can be well spent. Here, you can discover the widest range of authoritative, nonprofit information on all significant health problems. Some of the highlights include:

Medical and social science research

Prevention of outbreaks of infectious disease, including immunization services

Food and drug safety

Medicare (health insurance for elderly and disabled Americans) and Medicaid (health insurance for low-income people)

Better maternal and infant health

Head Start (preschool education and services)

Prevention of child abuse and domestic violence

Substance abuse treatment and prevention

Services for older Americans, including home-delivered meals

Comprehensive health services for Native Americans

- **Divorce Source (divorcesource.com)**. Divorce Source provides thoughtful information on custody, alimony, and support. Special categories you can click onto include: children and divorce, parental alienation, military and divorce, pensions and divorce, and divorce laws by state.

- **Foundation for Grandparenting (grandparents.com).**
Currently, two-and-a-half million grandparents are the sole
custodians of children of divorce. This website provides essential information on grandparent-child relationships and bond-
ing. It is a lively interactive website with categories you can
click onto regarding raising children (even a category on
step-grandparenting!).

- **Institute for Women's Policy Research (iwpr.org).** This
website is on "issues of poverty and welfare, employment and
earnings, work and family issues, the economic and social aspects
of health care and domestic violence, and women's civic and
political participation." It offers forums on family issues and
interviews and webcasts on subjects such as "marriage promotion
and welfare reform." Its press release section is a source of vital
information on family matters.

- **The National Center on Fathers and Families (ncoff
.upenn.edu).** This website—established by the Graduate School
of Education, University of Pennsylvania—is dedicated to
expanding knowledge about father involvement with children
and family development. Its objective is to improve the well-
being of children and it offers effective advice on the father's
involvement needed to create healthy families. As stated on the
site, "father's presence matters in terms of economic well-being,
social support, and child development."

- **Parents Without Partners (parentswithoutpartners.org).**
Parents Without Partners is one of the oldest, most reputable
divorce organizations. It is an excellent source of mutual support
for all divorced persons who want to break out of the loneliness
trap.

- **Stepparenting (parentsoup.com).** This is a lively interactive website that includes online community and message board connections for stepparents. Helpful information on stepparenting issues is available.

Websites for Helping Make the World a Better Place for You and Your Family

Successful ACDs are devoted to expanding their horizons. Their drive is to enrich their own and their family's entire life. These websites are directed toward that end and were recommended by members of our ACD groups

Counter-Conventional Wisdom Websites

The intent of the following two websites is not to brainwash you, but to stimulate a healthy skepticism in how you view the issues of the day that affect our own and our family's lives.

- **Alternet (alternet.org).** This is an online magazine that is similar in thoughtful news content to Common Dreams News Center (see next website listed), but more interactive. Interactive forums, discussion groups, and chat rooms enliven the participatory nature of this website.

- **Common Dreams News Center (commondreams.org).** This website provides a listing of provocative articles on current events. It is updated daily and offers comprehensive listings of television and radio news programs, periodicals, news services, and a special section on daily Washington developments. Common Dreams News Center is designed to make the visitor think more deeply about current national and world events.

Political Action Information

To flourish, healthy families need an environment in which everyone is free to speak one's mind and exercise one's vote. Families cannot flourish in an atmosphere of intimidation, racial and sexual discrimination, and arbitrary legal activity. Our Bill of Rights proudly proclaims these facts to the world. The following websites are useful guardians of these precious democratic rights.

- **American Civil Liberties Union (aclu.org).** This website is designed to protect the rights of everyone in our society to speak freely, regardless of race, color, creed, or gender.

- **Amnesty International (amnesty.org).** This organization is actively engaged in the protection of human rights throughout the world.

- **Gray Panthers (graypanthers.org).** We are all growing older and this website is a tonic for keeping us healthy, vibrant, and youthful. It vigorously fights age discrimination, which is so endemic in our society. It has stopped forced retirement at age sixty-five, exposed nursing home abuse, and promotes family security.

- **Judicial Watch (judicialwatch.org).** This is an objective, nonprofit public interest law firm's website that is dedicated to fighting government corruption.

- **League of Women Voters (lwv.org).** The slogan states "the personal is political." What happens politically in Washington,

D.C., affects our daily lives and determines to a great extent how well we can nurture ourselves and our children. A stable income, a decent wage, a fulfilling career, family health—all these issues that enable our families to flourish (or deteriorate if they are non-existent) depend to a significant degree on political decision-making. Our vote makes us the decision makers on these issues if we use it wisely. The League of Women Voters gives us the information we need. It is the best one-stop website for getting objective voting information. It lists detailed, comprehensive, nonpartisan election information on politicians and the issues voters can use to make informed voting decisions. Don't be misled by the title: this website is not gender biased. It is created for the effective use of both women and men.

• **National Association for the Advancement of Colored People (naacp.org).** The NAACP is the oldest established organization designed to protect African-Americans against any and all forms of discrimination.

• **The National Lawyers Guild (nlg.org).** This website is founded by an organization of lawyers dedicated to protecting the human rights of all individuals.

• **National Organization for Women (now.org).** The National Organization for Women is a key protector of women's rights and fights against all forms of discrimination against women.

Movies as Learning Tools

We are a nation of movie-goers, but the insights popular films can give regarding interpersonal relationships and family life are often overlooked. While we are entertained, we can also be educated, because many films can assist us in rethinking our value systems and how we behave with our families.

We often use popular films as teaching tools in our ACD groups to stimulate a greater understanding of interpersonal relationships, family life, divorce, and marriage.

The descriptions of the films we cite can be found in a superb website called the **Internet Movie Database** (imdb.com). This website is so popular it is visited by more than twelve million movie lovers every month. The films we recommend are available in either VHS or DVD formats (IMDB will tell you which format is available). We are always on the lookout to expand our list of movies-for-teaching, and you may wish to do so on your own. Here is a sampling of our list:

- *Affliction* shows the impact of alcoholism and physical abuse on family life and how it can damage the children, even though the parents never divorce.
- *A Beautiful Mind* provides accurate insights into mental illness and makes for understanding and compassion.
- *The Great Santini* shows how punitive authoritarian parenting can destroy children's self-esteem.
- *Minority Report* is set fifty years in the future, but really is about the present. This film offers a warning not to trust high-tech inventions to solve all of our problems, but trust in your own free will, not in brainwashing technical inventions, to provide the good life you wish to have.
- *Ordinary People* includes an excellent demonstration of how a child psychiatrist helps a depressed, suicide-prone adolescent overcome his depression.
- *Play It Again, Sam* is a very funny Woody Allen comedy about divorce and self-renewal. The moral is be

your authentic self, and you'll succeed in relationships. Don't pretend to be someone you are not.

- *Raisin in the Sun* shows how racial discrimination can destroy a family's security.
- *Scenes from a Marriage* is a superb examination by Ingmar Bergman about how a marriage can deteriorate even though on the surface everything seems fine. Divorce occurs because of the character's failure to communicate honestly and their misreading each other's motives and feelings.
- *The Thin Man* is more relevant today (in spite of an outdated approach toward liquor) even though it was made in 1934. This movie presents an ideal marriage: two people secure in their own identity, who respect each other and treat each other as equals. It is an ideal worth striving for today.
- *Traffic* is an excellent examination of how drugs can destroy the lives of middle-class children, even though the parents never divorce.
- *An Unmarried Woman* depicts self-renewal for a divorced woman after her husband left her.
- *The Way We Were* depicts how divorce can happen when two well-intentioned people are moving in separate directions because of the different value systems they hold.

A Note to the Reader

After reading a book whose ideas seem helpful, the next step is to put those ideas into practice in one's personal life. To help you in that endeavor, please feel free to contact us as follows:

The Creative Divorce, Love & Marriage Counseling Center
Phone: (415) 479-7636
Fax: (415) 472-2201
E-mail: melkr@aol.com

Index

kindness and empathy in, 101–2
open communication in, 104–6
personal responsibility in, 108–11, 112, 119
role modeling and, 49, 99–100
self-esteem building and, 111–17
validation of feelings in, 102–4
Parents Without Partners, 154
Permanent effect of first three years myth, 28–29
Permanent loser myth, 63–72, 141
Personal Intelligences, 30–31
Personal responsibility, 108–11, 112, 119, 138, 140, 147
Post-traumatic growth, 65
Poverty, 30, 38–39, 42, 44, 60, 130–31
Power-play game, 83–85
Power-struggle divorce, 6, 20–21
Prevailing, 137, 147
challenges to, 20–23
defined, 19
Prosperity, striving for, 119–20

Racial discrimination, 138–39, 141
Redbook, 27
Research findings, 25–36
on effect of first three years, 28–29
on intact families, 34–36
on multiple intelligences, 29–31
Resilience, x, xiii, xx, xxiv, 23, 33, 75, 79
defined, 19
importance of, 65–72
Resourcefulness, 120
Role models, xxiv, 107, 108, 109
new divorce, 31–34
parents as, 49, 99–100
for self-esteem, 100, 113
Roosevelt, Franklin D., 144–45
Royal Tenenbaums, The (film), xiii

San Francisco Chronicle, 33
Scientist in the Crib, The (Copnick, Meltzoff & Kuhl), 29
Second Chances (Wallerstein), 26
Self-empowerment
for divorced fathers, 56–58
Self-esteem, xxiii, 27, 40, 49, 83, 118
of divorced fathers, 58
effect of first three years on, 28

parental building of, 111–17
role models and, 100, 113
"Sex is everything" divorce, 10–11, 23
Sexual abuse, 38, 42, 43–44, 93, 113
Sexual-betrayal divorce, 7, 21
Shadow, 124
Single parents, 50, 57
Smith, Tom, 36
Spatial Intelligence, 30
Spouse abuse, 38, 138. *See also* Domestic violence
Stepparenting (website), 155
Stereotypes, 46, 47
of divorced fathers, 49
reality vs., 1–23
Stigmatization, ix, xiv, 141
Stone, Robert, 2–3
Strictness, 132–35
Success, striving for, 119–20
Suicide, 2, 112, 114
Surviving the Breakup (Wallerstein & Kelly), 26

Television, 64–65, 122. *See also* Media
Therapy. *See* Counseling
Three Ds (determination, discipline, dedication), 33
Time, xx, 26, 27
Time, importance of, 119
Togetherness trap, 83
Tolerance, 94–95
Twain, Mark, 140

Unexpected Legacy of Divorce, The (Wallerstein), 26
Unfinished business, 92–94
University of Chicago National Opinion Research Center, 36
University of Virginia, 25
USA Weekend, 32

Vengefulness, 13–16, 53–55
Visitation rights, 12, 49–50, 53–54, 59, 60
alternative terms for, 57–58
objection to terminology, 55–56

Wallerstein, Judith, 25–27
Websites, 151–57